One Hundred Years

at the Art Institute: A Centennial Celebration

The Art Institute of Chicago
MUSEUM STUDIES

VOLUME 19, NO. 1

One Hundred Years at the Art Institute: A Centennial Celebration

Foreword

One hundred years ago, the World's Columbian Exposition was in full swing, delighting and provoking visitors from around the world who ventured to Chicago to witness the progress of humankind. Among the visitors to the Fair was the historian Henry Adams, who declared in his autobiography that, "since Noah's Ark, no such Babel of loose and ill-joined, such vague and ill-defined and unrelated thoughts and half-thoughts and experimental outcries as the Exposition, had ever ruffled the surface of the Lakes." In Adams's view, "Chicago asked in 1893 for the first time the question whether the American people knew where they were driving."

The Art Institute of Chicago, as we know it today, was born at this turning point in American history. As the Columbian Exposition was closing in November 1893, the Art Institute moved into the acclaimed Beaux-Arts building on Michigan Avenue that had been built to house meetings, lectures, and other events of the Fair. The closing of the Columbian Exposition did not, however, bring to an end Chicago's role in presenting modern innovations to the world. Many artists who sought to reflect the chaotic and stimulating modern world that so shook Henry Adams at the Fair eventually found a receptive forum for their works in the galleries of the Art Institute.

As the essays in this issue of *Museum Studies* attest, the Art Institute has for generations confronted its visitors with the "experimental outcries" of the modernists, presenting art that has often confounded the expectations of the public. Long after Adams expressed astonishment over the impulses of modern man, the museum-going public and the leaders of the Art Institute continued to weigh the merits of the modern world as reflected in the art of this century.

Our first essay vividly portrays the incendiary impact of modern art on Chicago. Andrew Martinez, Assistant Archivist at the Art Institute, explores the story behind the Chicago showing of the famed 1913 International Exhibition of Modern Art—more widely known as the Armory Show—and its tumultuous reception. The Art Institute's version of the Armory Show featured some of the most controversial art of the European avant-garde, and the response of the public, the press, and even the students of the School of the Art Institute was often hostile. By examining many unpublished archival materials, Martinez provides a fresh view of the Art Institute's role in this risky venture.

One of the most ardent champions of modernism at the Art Institute was Daniel Catton Rich, director of the museum from 1938 to 1958. As John W. Smith, Archivist at the Art Institute, explains in his lucid essay, Rich came under attack for his vocal defense of modern art, but he never wavered in his conviction that the museum must educate the public about the art of its own time. Rich's influence, however, went beyond his interest in modernism, for in the two decades that he led the Art Institute he shaped or began many of the departments and activities that continue here to this day.

Our third essay tells the intriguing story of another controversial exhibition at the Art Institute—the 1949 showing of twentieth-century European art belonging to Louise and Walter Arensberg. Naomi Sawelson-Gorse of the University of California, Santa Barbara, tells the story of how the Arensbergs, with the help of artist Marcel Duchamp, put together one of the finest private collections of modern art anywhere, how the Art Institute arranged to display the collection in its galleries, and, finally, how the museum failed to secure the Arensbergs' works for its permanent collection. Sawelson-Gorse weaves together anecdotes, press accounts, and archival sources to tell a rich story.

The selection of archival photographs that begins this issue focuses our attention on the museum's roots in the World's Columbian Exposition. Many of these images have been collected and catalogued as part of the Art Institute's Digital Imaging Negative Project, which has been funded through a generous grant from the Samuel H. Kress Foundation. These photographs, in surveying forty years of the Art Institute's early activities and exhibitions, remind us that much has changed—from how a museum displayed art to how we once dressed and behaved—even as much has remained the same. As a number of these photographs show, the qualities that made the Art Institute's Michigan Avenue building so distinguished in 1893 remain in place a century later.

MICHAEL SITTENFELD
Editor

From the Archives: Photographs of The Art Institute of Chicago, 1893–1933

This special section of archival photographs documents the history of The Art Institute of Chicago from the completion of the Allerton Building in 1893 to the Century of Progress exhibition of 1933. In this forty-year span, the Art Institute grew in reputation and size to become, in many respects, the museum we know today. When the Art Institute moved into the Allerton Building on November 1, 1893, after fourteen years in other locations, it established itself on this site as one of the city's premier cultural institutions. And with the Century of Progress exhibition, the Art Institute proclaimed its stature as one of the world's finest museums.

In most instances, we have chosen these photographs as much for their visual appeal as for their documentary value. Our hope is that this selection evokes the spirit of the Art Institute during a crucial era of evolution and growth.

FIGURE 1. The Art Institute of Chicago under construction, c. 1892. The costs of building this structure were shared by the Art Institute and the World's Columbian Exposition. Before the Art Institute occupied this building, it was used during the World's Fair for meetings, lectures, and other events. It was designed by the Boston architectural firm Shepley, Rutan and Coolidge, and was later named the Robert Allerton Building after an important museum trustee. Following the World's Fair, this building housed not only the museum's galleries, but also The School of The Art Institute of Chicago. Photo by J. W. Taylor, courtesy of the Chicago Historical Society.

FIGURE 2. William M. R. French (1843–1914), a native of New Hampshire, was the first director of the Art Institute, from 1885 to 1914. As part of his duties, French also served as the Art Institute's first Curator of Painting and Sculpture and as director of the School of the Art Institute. During his tenure, French oversaw a series of exhibitions, particularly the annual exhibition of American painting and sculpture, that introduced Chicago audiences to the latest trends in art.

FIGURE 3. Charles L. Hutchinson (1854–1924) was the first president of the Art Institute's Board of Trustees, from 1882 until his death. Hutchinson, a wealthy and prominent Chicago financier, was president of the Corn Exchange National Bank, and he devoted much of his time to philanthropic causes. He believed that the Art Institute should be not only a repository for artworks, but also a tool for social reform and improvement. His vision helped transform the Art Institute into a great cultural institution. Photo courtesy of Mr. and Mrs. Carl T. Schuneman, Jr.

FIGURE 4. Front view of The Art Institute of Chicago, c. 1894.

FIGURE 5. Lobby of the Michigan Avenue entrance to the Art Institute, c. 1900, looking south into the galleries of Roman casts (the present location of the Museum Shop). In this photograph and the next (fig. 6), the lobby can be seen with its original mosaic floor and some of the numerous plaster casts that constituted the bulk of the museum's collection in its early days.

FIGURE 6. Lobby of the Michigan Avenue entrance to the Art Institute, c. 1900, looking north into the galleries of Renaissance casts (the present location of the coat check room and of gallery space devoted to prints and drawings). The sculpture in the right foreground is a plaster cast of a study for *The Republic* by Daniel Chester French, the brother of Art Institute Director William M. R. French (fig. 2). The final version of *The Republic* was a colossal gilded statue—it stood sixty-five feet tall—that greeted visitors to the Court of Honor at the World's Columbian Exposition.

FIGURE 7. An architectural sculpture class of the School of the Art Institute, 1895. During this era, the students of the School of the Art Institute often used the museum's plaster casts as inspiration for their own work, which included plaster and terracotta architectural ornamentation, mosaics, and ceramics.

FIGURE 8. A sculpture class of the School of the Art Institute, 1902.

FIGURE 9. Higinbotham Collection of plaster casts from Herculaneum and Pompeii, c. 1903. These casts were purchased in Italy for the Art Institute in 1893.

FIGURE 10. Bertha Honoré Palmer (1849–1918) was an important collector of Impressionist paintings, a prominent Chicago socialite, and the president of the Board of Lady Managers of the World's Columbian Exposition. After the death in 1902 of her husband, Potter Palmer, a Chicago real-estate magnate, she managed the family's business affairs. Through her friendship with artist Mary Cassatt, she became an early and ardent champion of Impressionism. Mrs. Palmer's bequest of paintings to the Art Institute formed the core of the museum's Impressionist works.

FIGURE 11. Martin A. Ryerson (1856–1932), one of the great art collectors of his time, served as a trustee (1890–1924) and as the vice president of the Art Institute (1901–24), and subsequently bequeathed over two hundred works to the museum. Ryerson, seen here in a 1904 photograph, took particular interest in paintings by Old Masters, Impressionists, and Post-Impressionists.

FIGURE 12. The Art Institute of Chicago, seen from Adams Street, c. 1904. This photograph was taken at a time when Michigan Avenue was narrower than it is now, and when the plaza in front of the Art Institute was more spacious. The famous bronze lions sculpted by Edward Kemeys (1843–1907) were moved closer to the building and to each other after plans were made in 1908 to widen Michigan Avenue. Photo by Barnes-Crosby, courtesy of the Chicago Historical Society.

FIGURE 13. Interior of the Art Institute's Blackstone Hall, c. 1905. Blackstone Hall was enormous, as can be seen in this photograph and the three that follow (figs. 14–16), and it housed more than 150 plaster casts. In many instances, the casts were painted to look as though they were made of bronze.

FIGURE 14. A drawing class of the School of the Art Institute in Blackstone Hall, c. 1908.

FIGURE 15. Interior of Blackstone Hall, c. 1905. Among the works on display in this photograph are casts of Robert Lelorrain's *Horses of the Sun* (at the mezzanine level), Antoine Coysevox's allegorical figures of the *River Garonne* and *River Dordogne* (both in Versailles), and a portion of a portal of the Cathedral of St. Etienne, Limoges.

FIGURE 16. Interior of Blackstone Hall, c. 1905. In the foreground is a cast of a portal from Notre Dame du Port at Clermont-Ferrand. In the background are casts of monumental equestrian sculptures by Donatello and Verrocchio.

FIGURE 17. A drawing class of the School of the Art Institute, c. 1910.

FIGURE 18. School children attending a drawing class at the Art Institute, c. 1915. At this time, the Chicago Board of Education and local museums, including the Art Institute, were engaged in a joint effort to introduce art to school children from Chicago and surrounding areas.

FIGURE 19. Hutchinson Gallery of Old Masters, December 1907. The center painting on the far wall is *Portrait of an Artist* (1644) by a follower of Frans Hals. The landscape at the center of the right wall is Meindert Hobbema's *Watermill with the Great Red Roof* (1670).

FIGURE 20. In 1908, the Art Institute displayed 655 Japanese woodblock prints on loan from Clarence Buckingham, Frederick William Gookin, and Frank Lloyd Wright, who designed this elegant exhibition. After Clarence Buckingham's death in 1913, his collection of almost 1,400 prints moved to the Art Institute, where they eventually became part of the permanent collection.

FIGURE 21. Japanese print exhibition designed by Frank Lloyd Wright, March 1908.

FIGURE 22. Washing one of the bronze lions in front of the Art Institute, c. 1930s.

FIGURE 23. A rally on the steps of the Art Institute to encourage enlistment in the United States' armed forces for duty in World War I, c. 1917.

FIGURE 24. Students of the School of the Art Institute on the second-floor south loggia of the Allerton Building, c. 1914.

FIGURE 25. View from the east of the Grand Staircase and second-floor galleries of the Allerton Building, c. 1911. In this view, the staircase is surrounded by modern French sculpture. In the background, paintings by Hubert Robert are visible. The original plans for the Grand Staircase called for an elaborately decorated dome that was never constructed. Nonetheless, generations of visitors to the Art Institute have been drawn to this space by the natural light that fills it.

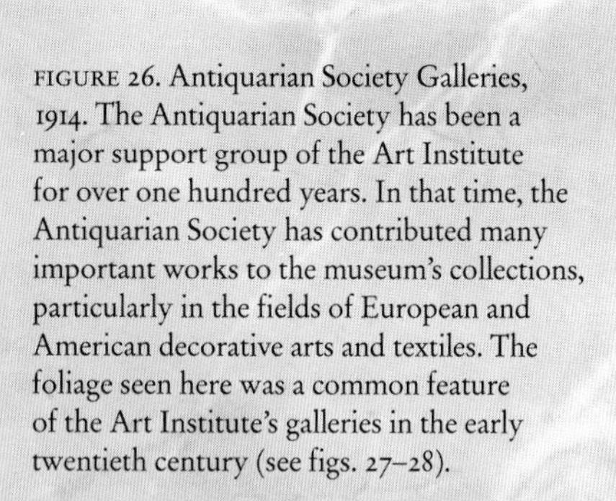

FIGURE 26. Antiquarian Society Galleries, 1914. The Antiquarian Society has been a major support group of the Art Institute for over one hundred years. In that time, the Antiquarian Society has contributed many important works to the museum's collections, particularly in the fields of European and American decorative arts and textiles. The foliage seen here was a common feature of the Art Institute's galleries in the early twentieth century (see figs. 27–28).

FIGURE 27. Among the many organizations, clubs, and societies that organized special exhibitions in conjunction with the Art Institute was the Women's National Farm and Garden Association, which sponsored this exhibit in March and April 1921. Other organizations that held exhibitions at the museum during this time included the American Bookplate Society, the Chicago Camera Club, the Friends of Our Native Landscape, the Chicago Aquarium Society, the Art Students' League, and the Chicago Society of Miniature Painters.

FIGURE 28. Twenty-Ninth Annual Chicago Architectural Exhibition, 1916. For more than thirty years, the Art Institute held an annual exhibition of architectural drawings, photographs, and models organized by the Chicago Architectural Club (1894–1922) and then the Chicago Architectural Exhibition League (1923–28). The 1916 exhibition included works by Holabird and Root; McKim, Mead and White; and other important architects of the time.

FIGURE 30. Lucy Maud Buckingham Memorial Gothic Room, 1924. The collection of medieval sculpture, tapestries, and decorative arts on display in this gallery was assembled by Kate Buckingham in honor of her sister. The Art Institute installed a number of period rooms during the 1920s, including galleries in British, French, Dutch, and American styles.

FIGURE 29. Top of Grand Staircase, October 1920. This photograph was taken during the exhibition of murals by the Czech artist Alphonse Mucha (1860–1939). Two of Mucha's murals can be seen in the background. The sculpture in the foreground is *Primitive Man* by the American artist Paul Wayland Bartlett (1865–1925).

FIGURE 31. Gallery with Spanish paintings, 1924. At the center of this room is the Art Institute's most significant Old Master painting, El Greco's *Assumption of the Virgin* (1577), which entered the museum's collection in 1906.

FIGURE 32. Museum guards at the foot of the Grand Staircase during the Century of Progress exhibition, 1933. The Art Institute's "Exhibition of Paintings and Sculpture," which ran from June 1 to November 1, 1933, was part of the Century of Progress Exposition that celebrated the centennial of the founding of Chicago. Displaying art from the thirteenth to the twentieth centuries, the exhibition was a phenomenal success, attracting over 1.5 million visitors to the museum. Events and exhibitions related to the Century of Progress Exposition at the Art Institute continued into 1934.

FIGURE 33. Eleanor Roosevelt at a ceremony honoring Jules Breton's *Song of the Lark* (1884) during the Century of Progress exhibition, July 10, 1934. *The Song of the Lark* was voted the most popular painting in America in a contest conducted by the *Chicago Daily News.*

FIGURES 34, 35. Among those who attended the Century of Progress exhibition were actor Edward G. Robinson, seen here looking at George Bellows's *Dempsey and Firpo* (1924; Whitney Museum of American Art, New York), and violinist Jascha Heifetz, seen here studying Vincent van Gogh's *Portrait of Joseph Roulin* (1888; Museum of Fine Arts, Boston).

FIGURE 36. Left to right, Art Institute Vice-President Chauncey McCormick, Mrs. Herbert Hoover, Mrs. Richard, and Art Institute Director Robert B. Harshe, looking at a replica of Gilbert Stuart's *George Washington* (1796) during the Century of Progress exhibition, 1933. The original version of Stuart's painting, known as the "Lansdowne" portrait, is owned by Lord Rosebery and is on long-term loan to the National Portrait Gallery, Washington, D.C.

FIGURE 37. Art Institute Lecturer Dudley Crafts Watson and a group of Gold Star Mothers standing before James McNeill Whistler's *Arrangement in Gray and Black: Portrait of the Painter's Mother* (1872; Musée du Louvre, Paris) during the Century of Progress exhibition, 1933.

FIGURE 38. The last-minute crowd at the Century of Progress "Exhibition of Paintings and Sculpture," November 1, 1933. This photograph was taken at 11:00 P.M. on the final day of the exhibition, just as the galleries were about to close. On the previous day, the exhibition attracted 44,442 visitors, which was the largest single-day attendance during the run of the show.

FIGURE 39. Michigan Avenue entrance to the Art Institute, looking north, during the Century of Progress exhibition, 1933.

A Mixed Reception for Modernism: The 1913 Armory Show at The Art Institute of Chicago

ANDREW MARTINEZ
Assistant Archivist
The Art Institute of Chicago

The cubists are coming, ho, ho, ho, ho;
The cubists are coming, ho, ho, ho, ho;
The cubists are coming from stately Manhattan;
The cubists are coming, ho, ho.

The art director has gone before,
He's said goodbye for a month or more;
The cubists are coming, and that's enough;
He cannot stand the futurist stuff.[1]

With insipid verse and inflammatory prose, the Chicago press heralded the coming of the International Exhibition of Modern Art, more commonly known as the Armory Show, to The Art Institute of Chicago in March 1913 (see fig. 1). As the first major exhibition of avant-garde art held in this country, the show had taken New York by storm the month before, introducing the nation to the works of Post-Impressionists, such as Vincent van Gogh, Paul Cézanne, and Paul Gauguin, and their immediate European successors, up to and including the Fauves and the Cubists. Organized by the Association of American Painters and Sculptors, the International Exhibition included works by contemporary American artists, but its notoriety was due to its focus on the most recent, "radical" innovations of European modernism.

While on view in New York, from February 17 through March 15, 1913, at the 69th Regiment Armory—from which the show took its more familiar name—the International Exhibition received an enormous amount of coverage from the local and national press. Although media accounts of the Association's enterprise were initially favorable, as the exhibition continued they became less flattering, characterizing the painting and sculpture of the Europeans as the work of degenerates and charlatans. Several Chicago newspapers sent correspondents to New York to cover the show, and their adverse dispatches, illustrated with reproductions of modernist painting and sculpture, appeared in the daily papers. As the opening at the Art Institute approached, the negative reviews continued, creating nervous anticipation and an atmosphere of intolerance in a city whose populace and press were hostile to the modern.

On March 20, 1913, four days before a scaled-down version of the New York show was to open at the Art Institute, the museum's director, William M. R. French (fig. 2), embarked for the West Coast on a combination lecture tour and vacation—a coincidence that was dutifully noted by the Chicago papers. French, by his own admission, did not appreciate the modernists, but his trip had been planned in November of 1912, before the museum ever became involved with the exhibition. And although he did not exactly flee from the International Exhibition of Modern Art as reported, he did not wel-

FIGURE 1. View of gallery 53 of the International Exhibition of Modern Art at The Art Institute of Chicago, 1913. The International Exhibition, which is more commonly known as the Armory Show, provided Americans with the most comprehensive gathering of art of the European avant-garde to date. After its initial showing at the 69th Regiment Armory in New York, the exhibition was on display at the Art Institute from March 24 to April 16, 1913. During this time, the show created a sensation among the Chicago press and public, and attracted 188,650 visitors to the museum. Among the artists represented in this gallery are Duchamp, Braque, Derain, Picasso, Archipenko, Duchamp-Villon, Gleizes, and Souza Cardoso. See fig. 14 for another view of this gallery.

FIGURE 2. William M. R. French, director of the Art Institute at the time of the International Exhibition, was reluctant to bring the show to the museum because of his skepticism about the artistic merit of much of its contents and his concern about the effect that the exhibition might have on the students of the School of the Art Institute. Despite his reservations, however, he did allow it to come to Chicago and insisted that it include a representative sample of the art of the European avant-garde.

come it either. French was hardly in the minority, for it would be some time before either the Art Institute, the city of Chicago, or the nation was able to accept this innovative but controversial art.

The fact that modernism was not readily received in the United States, or, more particularly, Chicago, is not surprising, since there were limited opportunities for the public to become familiar with some of the more recent developments in European painting and sculpture. Twenty years before the Armory Show, works by Impressionists such as Cassatt, Degas, Manet, Monet, Pissarro, Renoir, Rodin, and Sisley had been displayed in the Art Palace of the World's Columbian Exposition of 1893, Chicago's most significant international art exhibition to that date.

It was at the 1893 Exposition that Chicago attorney Arthur Jerome Eddy (fig. 3) became acquainted with the work of Whistler and Rodin. Eddy's fascination with these two artists subsequently led him to Europe, where he met them and commissioned portraits from them. Eddy shared his firsthand knowledge of these artists with the public through illustrated lectures he presented at the Art Institute and also through his book *Recollections and Impressions of James A. McNeill Whistler.*[2]

While incorporating Impressionism into the art-historical hierarchy, the city's official arbiters of taste—the Art Institute and its School—continued to cling to the conventions of academic art. In the years preceding the International Exhibition, the most advanced European painting that the Art Institute showed were examples of French Impressionism. In addition to an exhibition, "A Loan Collection of Selected Works of Modern Masters," featuring works by several Impressionists from the Durand-Ruel Gallery in New York, the museum also received loans from Bertha Honoré Palmer and Art Institute Vice-President Martin A. Ryerson, Chicago's two foremost collectors of French Impressionism. By 1913, Manet, Monet, and Rodin, as well as the expatriates Cassatt and Whistler, were represented in the museum's permanent collection.

Even more prevalent than the paintings of the French Impressionists were the works of contemporary American artists, many showing an Impressionist influence, that could regularly be seen in local galleries as well as in the collections of the Art Institute. The museum routinely held special exhibitions featuring examples by these Americans, as well.[3] Even the most radical groups of painters in the United States—the "Ashcan School" and "the Eight"—were represented in these exhibitions.

"The Eight" had their own show at the Art Institute in the fall of 1908. Although the vernacular, urban subject matter of this work somewhat dismayed museum director French, he did realize its significance and acknowledge that it was "worth having":

> "The Eight" present rather a remarkable appearance. Spectators generally are much perplexed by them. Nobody so far as I know expresses much favorable opinion. When artists deny themselves all the ordinary elements of pictorial art, regularity of composition, motives of beauty, all classic and conventional principles, and limit themselves to the expression of very limited range of actual fact, they cannot expect the world to sympathize with them. The penetrating critic can see that they know how to paint, but even he wonders why they do not do it.

French was particularly disappointed that one of "the Eight" was Arthur B. Davies (fig. 4), a former student of the School of the Art Institute. Davies would later become president of the Association of American Painters and Sculptors, and, in that capacity, was the principal organizer of its International Exhibition of Modern Art. Davies's art was less radical than his stance on art, which explains why he had a one-person show at the Art Institute in 1911 and why his work was acquired for the museum's permanent collection.[4]

In fact, almost one-third of the artists, most of whom were Americans, eventually included in the Chicago showing of the International Exhibition had previously exhibited at the Art Institute and would have been familiar to the viewing public. As extreme as some of these contemporary American artists may have seemed, there were even more radical developments taking place in the art of the nascent European avant-garde. And although the opportunities—short of a trip to the art centers of Europe, especially Paris—for Americans to see this modern art first hand were relatively scarce, they nevertheless did exist.

The most notable champion of modern art in the United States in the decade preceding the International Exhibition was the photographer and dealer Alfred Stieglitz. Beginning in 1908, Stieglitz, with the help of fellow photographer Edward Steichen, presented at his "291" gallery in New York the first American exhibitions of work by European artists such as Cézanne, Matisse, Picasso, and Henri Rousseau, and by American artists who had been to Europe and had been influenced by the modernists, including Hartley, Marin, and Weber. Chicagoans read about these events in an interview with Stieglitz in the December 11, 1911, *Chicago Evening Post,* in which he commented on the modernists and their reception in America. Stieglitz was not the sole purveyor of modernism, however, for other galleries in New York as well as in cities such as Boston, Chicago, Cleveland, Los Angeles, and Milwaukee were also displaying art by Americans working in a modernist vein.[5]

A show of works by the American artist Arthur Dove was presented at Chicago's W. Scott Thurber Gallery in March 1912, directly after its engagement at "291." Dove accompanied his works to Chicago and was on hand to take members of the press through the exhibition. Although some ridiculed Dove's work, others wrote favorable, perceptive reviews, making earnest attempts to understand the artist's intentions and, in turn, to explain them to their readers. Despite the good press, only one work was sold, not surprisingly, to Arthur Jerome Eddy. This purchase marked the beginning of his interest in collecting twentieth-century art.[6]

In January 1913, only two months before the arrival of the International Exhibition, the Art Institute hosted an "Exhibition of Contemporary German Graphic Art."

FIGURE 3. James McNeill Whistler (American, 1834–1903). *An Arrangement in Flesh Color and Brown (Arthur Jerome Eddy),* 1894. Oil on canvas; 209.5 x 92.7 cm. The Art Institute of Chicago, Arthur Jerome Eddy Memorial Collection (1931.501). A Chicago attorney, Eddy first saw Whistler's art at the World's Columbian Exposition in 1893. The following year, he met Whistler in Europe and commissioned this portrait. Eddy purchased eighteen paintings and seven lithographs from the International Exhibition, including works by Marcel Duchamp and Francis Picabia, two of the show's most radical artists.

Included were works by Beckmann, Corinth, Feininger, Kandinsky, Kollwitz, Marc, Nolde, and Pechstein. Oddly enough, this exhibition seems to have escaped the wrath of the press and public; but a show that opened in February, an "Exhibition of Contemporary Scandinavian Art," was not as fortunate.

Although the Scandinavian exhibition did contain works that could be considered Post-Impressionist, including six paintings by Edvard Munch, none of the works were nearly as radical as those by the contemporary German artists just seen at the museum or as those by the Fauves and the Cubists in the upcoming International Exhibition. However, some members of the Chicago press, anticipating the International Exhibition but not very knowledgeable about the art and artists it included, saw the Scandinavian show as representative of the new movements in art and seized the opportunity to attack them.

On February 27, the *Chicago Inter-Ocean* sounded the alarm with the headline "'Futurists' Startle by Hideous Lines. . .Scandinavian Painters Do Not Inspire a Happy Mood. Devoid of Color and Charm." Amy L. Paulding, author of the accompanying article, described the art as "weird, colorless, absolutely lacking in everything that is usually associated with the original conceptions of art; hideous delineations which look as if they were conceived in a nightmare and executed in a delirium."[7]

FIGURE 4. Arthur B. Davies, president of the Association of American Painters and Sculptors, was responsible for organizing the International Exhibition. Photo courtesy of the Armory Show Files, Joseph H. Hirshhorn Foundation Papers, Collection Archive, Hirshhorn Museum and Sculpture Garden, Smithsonian Institution.

The Scandinavian Exhibition became even more controversial when the Art Institute removed, "on moral grounds," the painting *Summer Days,* depicting poultry in a sunlit garden, by the Norwegian Bernhard Folkestad. Since no illustrations or descriptions of this work seem to exist, we do not know what people found objectionable. The *Chicago Daily Tribune,* while choosing not to describe the painting in more than "generalities," reported that, although some saw the public reaction as "silly prudishness," others were shocked, and that "most of the women hurried away from it after the first glance." When French became aware of the problem, he "ordered the picture 'down and out' or rather down in the basement. . .[to] gather. . .dust."[8]

Three days after this incident, Chicago's official art censor, Sergeant Jeremiah O'Connor, impounded a reproduction of Paul Chabas's *September Morn* from an art store window. The image showed a naked young woman standing ankle deep in water, modestly trying her best, considering the circumstances, to cover herself. O'Connor claimed to have acted on the orders of Mayor Carter H. Harrison and, in his own defense, stated that "the picture is not conducive to good morals. It may be a work of art, but its moral tone is questionable. I believe that the only proper place for it is in the Art Institute, and not in the display window on Wabash Avenue." Local artists condemned O'Connor's actions and eventually the issue was tried in court.[9] Meanwhile, the *Chicago Daily Tribune* posed the question, "When is art art? When wicked?," and the *New York Telegraph* speculated that a general ban on displaying images of nudes might precipitate a police raid on the Art Institute.[10]

This lack of sophistication about modern art and the apprehension that many felt toward it were what the Association of American Painters and Sculptors hoped to redress in presenting the International Exhibition of Modern Art. Formed late in 1911, the Association saw the need to shock America out of its artistic provincialism and complacency and to create more hospitable venues for showing the works of its members, as well as art by other modern artists.[11]

The Association wasted no time in trying to organize an exhibition. By late January 1912, its secretary, artist Walt Kuhn (fig. 5), was writing to various American museums, including The Art Institute of Chicago, to inquire whether they would be willing to hold an exhibition of works by members of the Association. French's reply could not have been too encouraging: "Our President, Mr. Hutchinson, and I conferred upon the matter, and all I can say is that our attitude toward your society is friendly, but we cannot arrange any additional exhibitions here for sometime to come."[12] The Art Institute's exhibition schedule may indeed have been full, but it is also likely that French and Hutchinson did not feel the need to hold yet another exhibition of contemporary American artists in addition to the museum's annual shows.

Soon after these initial inquiries, perhaps because of unfavorable responses like the Art Institute's, the Association abandoned this particular project. By April 1912, efforts were under way to rent the 69th Regiment Armory in New York City for a larger show that would include European art, but it was not until late in the summer that this alternate exhibition began to take shape. It was then that Arthur B. Davies saw the catalogue for the Cologne Sonderbund exhibition, which showcased the modernists and Post-Impressionists. It featured one hundred twenty-five works by van Gogh, twenty-six by Cézanne, twenty-five by Gauguin, and sixteen by Picasso; it also included a historical section of nineteenth-century precursors to modernism.[13] Davies decided that the Association's exhibition should be modeled after this show, and he sent the catalogue to Kuhn. Kuhn, realizing the urgency of the matter, quickly set sail for Europe and arrived in Cologne just in time to see the Sonderbund exhibition on its closing day.

Kuhn spent the following weeks traveling through Germany, the Netherlands, and France, meeting with dealers, collectors, and artists to secure loans for the International Exhibition, while also receiving a crash course on modern art. On October 25, he arrived in

FIGURE 5. Walt Kuhn, secretary of the Association of American Painters and Sculptors, traveled to Europe to select works for the International Exhibition. He was in Chicago during the exhibition at the Art Institute, and was disappointed with the unfavorable reception it received from both press and public. Photo courtesy of the Armory Show Files, Joseph H. Hirshhorn Foundation Papers, Collection Archive, Hirshhorn Museum and Sculpture Garden, Smithsonian Institution.

FIGURE 6. Walter Pach, European representative for the Association of American Painters and Sculptors, acted as the sales representative for the International Exhibition in New York and Chicago. Photo courtesy of the Armory Show Files, Joseph H. Hirshhorn Foundation Papers, Collection Archive, Hirshhorn Museum and Sculpture Garden, Smithsonian Institution.

FIGURE 7. Arthur T. Aldis, Chicago arts patron and governing member of the Art Institute, was most responsible for bringing the International Exhibition to Chicago. He met Davies and Kuhn (figs. 4 and 5) in Europe while they were selecting works for the show, and told them that the Art Institute would host the exhibition after it closed in New York. At a time when patrons played a major role in shaping museum exhibitions, he was able to persuade the Art Institute to commit itself to this revolutionary enterprise. Photo courtesy of the Chicago Historical Society, Gift of the Commercial Club of Chicago, 1922.

Paris where, on November 6, Davies joined him. Through the help of the American painter and critic Walter Pach (fig. 6), a resident of Paris and soon to be the Association's European representative, Davies and Kuhn met the collectors and salon hosts Gertrude and Leo Stein and visited several artists in their studios, including Constantin Brancusi, the Duchamp-Villon brothers, and Odilon Redon.

Also in Paris, Davies and Kuhn were introduced to Chicagoan Arthur T. Aldis (fig. 7), which proved to be fortuitous for the Art Institute. Active in the affairs of the museum as a governing member and a director of the Friends of American Art auxiliary organization, Aldis became the Association's greatest ally in Chicago. He took an immediate interest in the International Exhibition and promised Davies and Kuhn that the Art Institute would host the show after it closed in New York.[14] For Aldis to commit the museum to the exhibition without consulting either its director or trustees indicates that he must have enjoyed tremendous influence at the museum and was confident in his ability to get things done.

Exactly how Aldis effected a decision on the part of the Art Institute to take the International Exhibition is not known. French claimed that the trustees allowed him and Charles Hutchinson, president of the board, to do as they thought best concerning exhibitions, but during the greater part of the period that the International Exhibition was arranged and exhibited at the Art Institute, Hutchinson and Vice-President Martin A. Ryerson were traveling abroad.[15] This does not mean that, in this period, French was acting on his own, for throughout the negotiations for the International Exhibition, he often stated that he was following instructions from the Art Committee, comprised of several trustees and officers, including French, who met infrequently and settled matters by informal conferences.

The Art Committee's discussions about the International Exhibition were not recorded. The exhibition apparently did not require any official motion or vote by the full Board of Trustees, for there is no mention of the show in the board's minutes prior to its arrival in Chicago. It eventually became clear that French and several trustees were against having the show, but, even with this opposition, Aldis got the museum to commit to this exhibition of considerable cost and magnitude with less than five-months' notice. This was a time when individual trustees and patrons played an aggressive role in shaping the collections and exhibitions of American art museums. As his subsequent correspondence with the Art Institute and the Association indicates, Aldis certainly made his presence felt.[16]

Arthur Taylor Aldis and his wife, Mary, were well-known patrons of the arts in Chicago. Born in Vermont, Aldis earned college and law degrees from Harvard University and, in 1889, moved to Chicago, after working for five years as a rancher in Wyoming. He was soon heading the real-estate firm of Aldis and Company. At their country residence in Lake Forest, Illinois, the Aldises established an artists' colony called "The Compound." There, in 1910, Mary started the Aldis Playhouse, a predecessor to the "little theater" movement, where plays were presented by contemporary European and American playwrights, including her own works. While Mary devoted her energies to the theater both in Chicago and on the East Coast, her husband frequently traveled abroad in Europe and Africa.[17]

Aldis was very familiar with Paris, where his brother, Owen Franklin Aldis, lived with his wife, the Countess Marie Madeleine Dumas. On his visits, Aldis frequented art galleries and became acquainted with both artists and dealers. At the time he met Davies and Kuhn, Aldis attended the Salon d'Automne, which featured works by many of the European and American modernists, including some that the two American artists were trying to secure for the International Exhibition. So Aldis had a good idea of what the show would contain.

From Paris, Davies and Kuhn went on to London to arrange more loans and to view critic Roger Fry's second exhibition at the Grafton Gallery, a sequel to his first landmark show in England of Post-Impressionist and modern art.[18] For dealers considering an untested American market, it must have been reassuring to know that there would be more than one venue for the exhibition, and having the imprimatur of an established art museum such as the Art Institute was most likely beneficial to the Association in securing loans. Davies and Kuhn, enthused by all they had seen and accomplished in Europe, returned to the United States predicting great success for their project. Aldis, for his part, saw to it that Chicago would participate in this momentous event.

Soon after returning home, Aldis contacted French about the International Exhibition as well as about an exhibition of contemporary Spanish painters.[19] Although French considered Aldis "rather wild and radical in his taste, and precipitate in his actions," he promptly looked into both exhibitions.[20]

Knowing nothing about the International Exhibition other than what Aldis had told him, French wrote on November 19, 1912, to James B. Townsend, president of the New York-based journal *American Art News*, for more information:

> One of our friends talks to me about some projected exhibition to be held in New York, apparently of foreign pictures of the most modern description. Understands that a large fund has been raised for the purpose. Supposes I know all about it, as it has been talked of in all the papers, etc. I have read Art Notes faithfully, but I do not remember seeing anything about this.[21]

Although Townsend's reply was informative, it surely could not have given French a favorable first impression of the enterprise:

> Your informant probably had in mind the display that has been planned by the newly formed Society of American Painters and Sculptors and which is to be held in a large armory here, Feb. 15–March 15. This exhibition is really in opposition to the Academy of Design, and is being run by Gutzon Borglun [*sic*], Leon Dabo and Arthur B. Davies—all of whom, as you know, are trouble makers. It will be a good show, however, as they have sent Davies and Walt Kuhn to Europe to get all the "freak" pictures, sculptures, etc., possible, to represent what they call "The Modern Movement in France and Germany."[22]

Apparently undeterred, French wrote to the Association on November 27 to begin negotiations for the International Exhibition. Because Davies and Kuhn were almost solely responsible for the administration of the exhibition and were overwhelmed with the arrangements for the New York show, now less than two months away, neither French nor Aldis, who was also corresponding with Davies and Kuhn, made much progress in arranging a Chicago showing.

While in New York in early January 1913, French conducted business with Davies and Kuhn in person. By January 13, French had returned to Chicago and had reported the results of his trip to Hutchinson, who scheduled a meeting of the Art Committee to discuss the exhibition. Although a contract was far from being realized, it was apparent that the Art Institute was fully committed to hosting the International Exhibition. On January 14, before the Art Committee met, French wrote to Davies that if "it becomes necessary for you to reach decisions, you can state to the association that the Art Institute will be glad to exhibit such part of the collection as you can send and we can accommodate."[23] The shipping and installation of exhibitions must have been much less complicated in those days than they are today, because French requested the exhibition for March 25, ten days after its closing in New York and the same day that two other exhibitions were scheduled to begin at the Art Institute!

On February 17, 1913, the International Exhibition of Modern Art officially opened in New York with over one thousand works of art. The media praised the Association for realizing an exhibition of such tremendous scale, but it was less than enthusiastic about the painting and sculpture of the European Post-Impressionists, finding the works of the Americans rational and sober in comparison. Harriet Monroe, founder of *Poetry Magazine* and art critic for the *Chicago Daily Tribune,* attended the press preview on February 16. Her review of the exhibition, while appearing under the headlines "Art Show Open to Freaks" and "American Exhibition in New York Teems with the Bizarre," was more favorable than most:

> It is a live show, this International Exhibition. . . . It has the air of cosmopolitanism never before attained in this country except at world's fairs, and it is less bound by academic standards. . . .
>
> Even the cubists seem to be playing interesting games with kaleidoscopic polygons of color; even Matisse is dancing a wild tango on some weird barbarous shore. We cannot always tell what they mean, but at least they are having a good time. . . .

The American exhibits, which outnumber the others, hold their own with complete assurance. Many of them come from radicals whom more conservative exhibitions have not appreciated. . . .

Most American exhibitions are dominated by the conservatives. Not so this one; the radicals are in control, and there are new voices in the chorus. . . .

Thus it is fortunate that Chicago is to see part of the exhibition. Arrangements are now complete for sending half of the exhibition to Boston and half to the Art Institute after the close of the show in New York.[24]

Aldis, unaware that Boston had also requested the exhibition, was alarmed by this latest development. Wishing to protect the Art Institute's interests, he sent an anxious letter to Kuhn, revealing a provincialist bias as well as a proselytizer's zeal:

I see by this morning's paper that your exhibition in New York is to be divided between Chicago and Boston.

Please be sure to give us a "square deal" in this. We were first to ask to come in. Let us have our full half of Cézanne, Gaguin [*sic*], Van Gogh, Matisse, and Picasso, et al., which our students and our public here would not otherwise have a chance to see. Boston is a seaport and a third nearer Europe, besides which Mr. Davies told me that the heart and genius of American Art were situated in the Middle West. Therefore, let's make 'em throb![25]

Aldis concluded by saying that he would come to New York soon to see the show. On February 19, 1913, Kuhn wrote to Aldis to assure him of a "square deal" and to inform him that French was at the exhibition and "in the hands of Mr. Davies."[26]

It seems that French's visit to the Armory reinforced his previous misgivings about the International Exhibition, and about modern art in general. On his return train ride to Chicago, French recorded his impressions of the exhibition, along with a description of the installation, to be sent to Hutchinson in Europe (see Appendix at the end of this essay for the full text of French's letter):

The fraction of the exhibition comprising the real modernists—the post-impressionists, cubists, pointillists, futurists—six or seven galleries, is eminently satisfactory. Anything more fantastic it would be hard to conceive. Some of the works are mere unmeaning assemblages of forms, with gay color, conveying no idea whatever, but bearing such titles as "Dance" or "Souvenir." A few, more logically, have no titles, but merely numbers. As an appeal to curiosity this part of the show is a decided success. Sculpture does not lend itself to idealism of this class, and the statues are clearly explicable, sometimes good in spirit, but generally exaggerated or distorted. . . .I suspect we have here the representatives of the two classes of radicals. First, a few eccentrics, some of them, like Van Gogh, actually unbalanced and insane, who really believe what they profess and practice; secondly, the imitators, who run all the way from sheer weakness to the most impudent charlatanism. The choice is between madness and humbug. How then should these artists have admirers among reasonable people! . . .With regard to the desirability of bringing the exhibition to Chicago, my opinion has changed. I at first thought it would be a good thing to satisfy the curiosity of the public, and as I visited the exhibition for the first time I felt a sort of exhilaration in the absurdity of it all. I still think it would be reasonable and right for us to exhibit a single gallery, perhaps fifty examples, of the most extreme works, so that our public may know what they are. But when it comes to bringing a large part of the exhibition here (we could accommodate about one-half), to incurring great expense, to turning the Art Institute upside down, . . . I hesitate. We cannot make a joke of our guests. It becomes a serious matter. As I visited the exhibition repeatedly I became depressed, to think that people could be found to approve methods so subversive of taste, good sense and education; of everything that is simple, pure, and of good report.

French concluded by singling out and assessing several of the European artists:

Matisse's work: If this work were submitted to me without explanation, I should regard it as a joke. It is asserted that he is an accomplished painter. I have never seen anything to show it, and I am of the opinion that if he ever did anything really distinguished it would now be exhibited. I think it probable that Matisse, failing to distinguish himself in regular lines, resorted to this work to attract attention. Certainly the work is without merit. It has no subtlety of line, no sweetness of color, no refinement of sentiment, no beauty of any kind.

Redon's work: This work gives more impression of a sincere but unbalanced mind. It is not without beauty and evidences of training, and yet it is irrational. Some of the flower painting, which is much admired, appears to me poor and ineffectual. Davies' work is somewhat akin to this, but technically better. . . .

Van Gogh's work: Not so good as I expected from some prints I have seen. Other people have done the same things better. It is well known that he was violently insane.

Duchamp and Picabia: The wildest of the cubists. Humbugs—not incapable.

Gauguin: Heavy and ugly.[27]

In hindsight, one is tempted to characterize William French as a reactionary or a philistine, unable to recognize the talent of these artists or appreciate what are now considered to be some of the seminal works of modernism.[28] Yet French, then sixty-nine years old, was an experienced art reviewer and lecturer and had been associated with the Art Institute's museum and school for over thirty years. His attitudes were not only consistent with what one would expect from the director of an established art school and museum—one whose job it was to teach and maintain accepted ideas and standards of "Truth" and "Beauty"—but also paralleled the tastes of the time.

French's younger brother, the noted sculptor Daniel Chester French, also visited the International Exhibition in New York and was equally unimpressed by what he saw. When Pach, acting as sales representative for the Association as well as Daniel French's guide through the Armory, compared Cézanne's handling of form to that of Giotto and the Italian Primitives, the sculptor replied, "I don't see that the Primitives, with the state of ignorance of the time when they lived, are any excuse for a man's doing the same thing today."[29] Although Pach attributed this aversion to modernism as being characteristic of an older generation, even those who made an earnest attempt to comprehend the new movements found them difficult to understand.

To accuse William French and his contemporaries of being anachronistic fails to take into account just how novel the works in the International Exhibition truly were. Pach himself struggled for more than half a year to reach a tentative understanding of Matisse's art, and Walt Kuhn experienced similar difficulties coming to terms with the paintings of Cézanne.[30] As his letter to Hutchinson indicates, French, too, was ambivalent about modernism, as well as the merits of the exhibition. His statements that he found the modernist section "eminently satisfactory" and the exhibition, as a whole, exhilarating, contradict his assessment of modern art as "madness and humbug" and his feelings of depression when contemplating the possible acceptance of the new art by the public. But as perplexed as French was by what he had seen at the Armory, he must have understood at some level the significance of the exhibition since, despite his hesitations, he did not resist bringing it before the public in Chicago.

After French had left New York, Newton H. Carpenter, the Art Institute's business secretary, stayed behind to negotiate a contract with the Association. Since French planned on being on the West Coast and Hutchinson was already abroad, the administration of the International Exhibition at the Art Institute was entrusted to Carpenter. Arthur Aldis and his friend George Porter, a fellow governing member at the museum, had also gone to New York to see the exhibition and were most likely involved in the negotiations.[31]

By February 28, 1913, a contract between the Art Institute and the Association was completed, with both parties agreeing to "do all they can to make the exhibition in Chicago as valuable and profitable to each other and the public as possible." According to the agreement, Davies was to select the works to be shown, subject to the final approval of French. The Art Institute was to pay $2,500 to the Association for the exhibition and would receive half of the profits from the sale of catalogues, photographs, and reproductions of the works exhibited. The Association was to provide its own sales agents and be the sole recipient of the proceeds from art sales. Should any officers of the Association come to Chicago to assist with the exhibition, both the Art Institute and the Association would split their travel and accommodation expenses. Finally, the Art Institute was to pay for the costs of insuring and transporting the art to and from Chicago and would also insure the works while at the museum.[32]

In the meantime, French had returned to Chicago to face the reception of the "Exhibition of Contemporary Scandinavian Art," which he described as "decidedly violent," and to try to arrange for adequate gallery space for the International Exhibition.[33] Left with no options other than taking down portions of the permanent collection and canceling previously scheduled exhibitions, French did his best to convince the scheduled exhibitors that they would benefit by not being associated with the modernists and portrayed himself and the museum as reluctant participants in the International Exhibition.[34]

On March 5, French wrote to Hutchinson in Paris, reiterating his previous assessment of the International Exhibition and reporting on the museum's current shows, including a "very refined exhibition of portraits of women" by John Alexander, president of the National Academy of Design, the organization with which the Association of American Painters and Sculptors was at odds. French was also delighted to inform Hutchinson of dissent within the Association, stating, "I am amused to learn that Gutzon Borglum, the Vice-President of the new Modernist Association in New York, has quarreled with Mr. Davies and the other officers, and resigned in a violent letter to the papers."[35]

While French apprised Hutchinson of the latest news, Aldis made his agenda known to Carpenter. In a letter of March 5, Aldis suggested that the opening date of the exhibition be moved forward one day, so that a fundraising reception could be held in the evening for Chicago "Society." More importantly, Aldis, lacking confidence in either French or Carpenter to properly install the exhibition, suggested that it be left to Davies and Kuhn:

> Proper exhibition of this very mixed collection is an important and difficult matter, and as I believe the date for its necessary closing in Chicago is fixed, every day saved in opening the exhibition is that much gained, as it adds nothing to the expense and would add something to the receipts and the public benefit.[36]

Ever the businessman, Carpenter would have found this last suggestion appealing. Not only was he arranging to have the exhibition catalogue printed in Chicago at a savings of twenty-five percent, but he was also busy publicizing the exhibition in press releases and interviews:

All of the best works of the sensational exponents of the post-impressionists, futurist and cubist schools of art will be represented at the International Art exhibition. . . .

I can not describe a cubist. . .but I told one of the girls in the sculpture class that if she built a group of clay and let me stand off and hurl a brick at it for a while it would be a cubist piece of sculpture when I was through. If it was painted it would represent a cubist composition.

As for the futurist? Well, I can not say. But let me tell you this, that there are so many good pictures in the show that by the time you have looked at them all you will forget the cubists, post-impressionists and the vagueists—my own term—and remember good art only. It's to be a great show. It's the biggest thing Chicago has had this season.[37]

Carpenter may not have been the most informed spokesman for the exhibition—fortunately for the Association, Kuhn and publicist Frederick James Gregg were also working with the Chicago press—but he did provide good copy. He also made sure that French was aware of Aldis's suggestions concerning the installation.

Nevertheless, French had his own ideas about what should be included to make the exhibition as practical as possible to the Chicago audience. Rather than abdicate all responsibility for an exhibition for which he did not care, French conveyed his vision of the International Exhibition to Davies in writing:

Of course what we especially want is the more novel part of the exhibition, chiefly the things which come from Europe. . . . We might limit the American exhibitors to one work apiece. Some of them are permanently represented in our collections, such as Henri, Hassam, Weir, Beal, C. H. Davis, Cassatt, Davies, H. D. Murphy, Bessie Potter, etc., and there seems no good reason for going to the expense of transporting their works hither. . . .

There is another section of the exhibition that may well be omitted, and it is a troublesome and expensive part. . . .I mean the old paintings by the radicals and reformers of other days. Our public is well acquainted with these works, and we have examples in our permanent collection of Courbet, Manet, Monet, Delacroix, Goya, Corot and many others. It seems unnecessary therefore to send these here.

With regard to the rest of the exhibition, we want the works of Matisse, Gauguin [see fig. 8], Redon, Duchamp, Cézanne, Picasso, Van Gogh, Rousseau, John and the rest of the well known and extraordinary foreigners.

Probably the foreign sculpture, about fifteen pieces, had better come.[38]

Though Davies has always been credited with selecting the works exhibited, French clearly had a say in defining the exhibition's parameters. And, to his credit, despite his personal aversion to the work of the European modernists, French strongly supported their inclusion in the Chicago exhibition, demonstrating an understanding of

FIGURE 8. Paul Gauguin (French, 1848–1903). *Head of a Tahitian with Profile of Second Head to His Right*, c. 1891–92. Black and red chalk, selectively stumped and fixed, on wove paper; 35.2 x 36.9 cm. The Art Institute of Chicago, Gift of Mrs. Emily Crane Chadbourne (1922.4794). This was one of four works on paper by Gauguin lent to the International Exhibition by Emily Crane Chadbourne, a Chicagoan and part-time resident of Paris. Until this time, few (if any) works by Gauguin had been exhibited in the United States. This drawing was one of several works displayed in Chicago that later entered the Art Institute's collection.

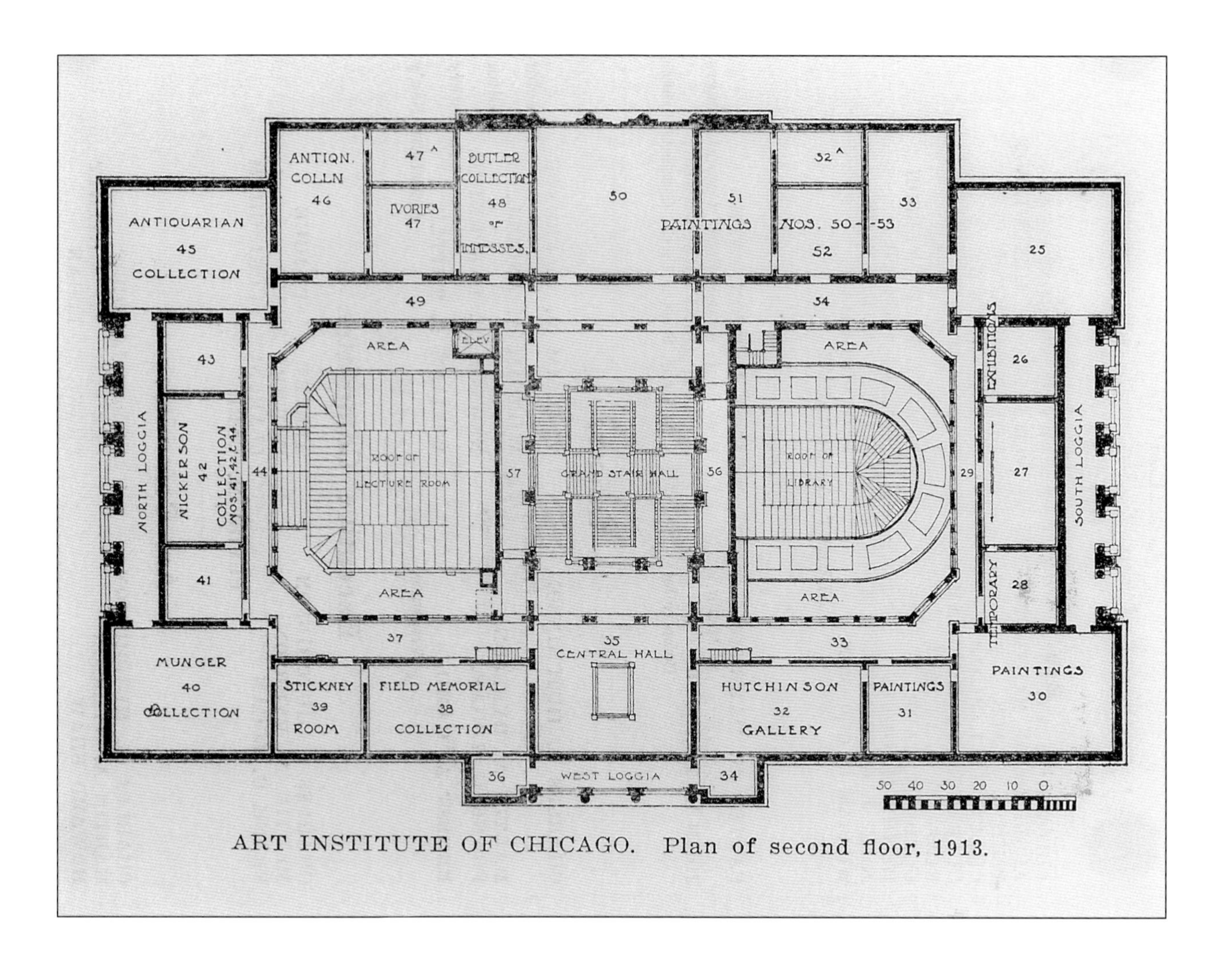

FIGURE 9. Plan of the second-floor galleries, The Art Institute of Chicago, 1913. With 634 works, the International Exhibition was held in galleries 25–26 and 50–54, as well as a space between gallery 50 and the top of the Grand Staircase (see upper right of this map). A portion of the installation can be seen in figs. 1 and 10–16.

the exhibition's educational aims and a sensitivity to the public's curiosity about the unknown European work.

On March 13, Davies submitted his final design for the exhibition at the Art Institute (see fig. 9). When the show was finally installed, the gallery designations varied slightly from Davies's written plans. The second-floor gallery at the top of the museum's grand staircase featured nine screens by the American painter Robert Chanler (figs. 10 and 11). Gallery 50 contained the works of some of the European modernists, including Bonnard, Denis, Segonzac, and Matisse (fig. 12). Gallery 51 was dedicated to works by English, Irish, German, and American painters. Gallery 52 was assigned to the Post-Impressionists Cézanne, Gauguin, van Gogh, and Rousseau (fig. 13), with gallery 53 designated for the Cubists (figs. 1 and 14). Galleries 25 (fig. 15) and 54 and, probably, 52A were reserved for the remainder of the American paintings. Thirty-seven works by Redon filled gallery 26 (fig. 16). It was decided that the sculpture in the exhibition would be dispersed throughout the galleries, and that some of the works on paper would be hung in the museum's print galleries.[39]

Aside from approving Davies's installation plans, French's participation in the planning of the exhibition had, at this point, mostly come to an end. The exhibition was in Carpenter's hands and, as its opening date approached (it was moved forward one day, as Aldis had requested, to the afternoon of Monday, March 24), he and several other Chicagoans were becoming increasingly nervous.

Arthur Jerome Eddy, whose law practice required him to live and work in both Chicago and New York, had seen the International Exhibition in New York and

FIGURES 10, 11. Two views of the entrance to the International Exhibition at the top of the Grand Staircase. On display in this space were screens by Robert Chanler and sculptures by Henri Matisse, Aristide Maillol, and Joseph Bernard.

FIGURE 12. View of gallery 50 of the International Exhibition. Works by Henri Matisse appear on the right wall. The large standing sculptural figures are by the German artist Wilhelm Lehmbruck. Among the smaller sculptures are works by the Romanian artist Constantin Brancusi.

FIGURE 13. View of gallery 52 of the International Exhibition. The major Post-Impressionists were featured in this gallery. On the left wall are paintings by Vincent van Gogh and on the right wall are paintings by Paul Cézanne. Works by Paul Gauguin were also displayed in this gallery.

FIGURE 14. View of gallery 53 of the International Exhibition. The second painting from the right, bottom row, is *Village (Rueil)* by Maurice de Vlaminck, and the fourth painting from the right, bottom row, is *Dances at the Spring* by Francis Picabia. Both were purchased by Arthur Jerome Eddy from the International Exhibition in New York. The painting by Vlaminck is now in the collection of the Art Institute as part of the Arthur Jerome Eddy Memorial Collection, and the painting by Picabia is now in the Louise and Walter Arensberg Collection of the Philadephia Museum of Art. See fig. 1 for another view of this gallery.

FIGURE 15. View of gallery 25 of the International Exhibition. Featured in this gallery were works by contemporary American artists. The painting on the right wall in the left corner, *Figure in Motion* by Robert Henri, depicting a standing nude woman, was the subject of much controversy. Henri's painting was deemed immoral by the press, the public, and even several of the Art Institute's trustees.

FIGURE 16. View of gallery 26 of the International Exhibition. This gallery featured works by the French artist Odilon Redon, who was virtually unknown in the United States at the time but proved popular among collectors who attended the exhibition.

FIGURE 17. André Derain (French, 1880–1954). *Forest at Martigues,* c. 1908. Oil on canvas; 82.6 x 100.3 cm. The Art Institute of Chicago, Arthur Jerome Eddy Memorial Collection (1931.506). Derain's *Forest at Martigues* was displayed in gallery 53 of the International Exhibition.

had purchased several works, including some of the most recent examples of European modernism (see fig. 17). On March 15, Eddy, in an effort to ensure that his patriotism would not be questioned while still cultivating his reputation as Chicago's most daring art collector, wrote to Davies and offered his own ideas regarding the Chicago installation:

> I have told Mr. French. . .that all the pictures I purchased would come on to Chicago, and that includes the painting by Kroll; two by Taylor and one by Manigault, all Americans. I particularly desire that these pictures be exhibited with the foreign pictures I purchased, because taken all together they illustrate my attitude in art, which is exceedingly catholic. While if the foreign pictures alone were exhibited, it would naturally give rise to the inference that I had lost interest in the strong virile American pictures. . . .
>
> It is needless to say that I also have in mind the fact that the exhibition of those American pictures will be of benefit to the artists who painted them.

Eddy also demonstrated his interest in making the art accessible to the public by requesting that the titles of all his pictures be translated into English.[40]

The galleries that would house the exhibition were emptied on March 15 and, by March 18, with the opening less than a week away and receptions already planned, Carpenter began to wonder when the exhibition would arrive and when he would receive a final draft of the catalogue that still had to be printed in Chicago (see fig. 18). Over the next few days, Carpenter sent several letters and telegrams daily to Davies and Kuhn. When the Association was not ignoring these pleas, it was offering rather vague answers.

By March 19, the first representative of the Association, publicist Frederick J. Gregg, had arrived in Chicago and was briefing the press. Gregg's decision to use the literary stylings of Gertrude Stein as an analogy for Cubist painting was probably a mistake, for the press had a field day parodying Stein's prose.[41] Kuhn and Pach arrived late in the evening on Friday, March 21, and, on Saturday morning, they were at the Art Institute to supervise the installation of six hundred and thirty-four works of art. With the help of the museum's installation crew, Gregg, and the artist Robert Chanler, Kuhn, and Pach managed to install everything but the sculpture by evening's end.[42]

On March 24, before the International Exhibition opened to the public, Frank G. Logan, the acting president of the Board of Trustees in Charles Hutchinson's absence, toured the galleries and was not entirely pleased with what he saw. Logan convened a meeting of the trustees to discuss "the propriety and policy of taking out some of the pictures offered, before the opening to the public." The three paintings singled out as being offensive were: *Spirit of Evil* by Gauguin, *Figure in Motion* by Henri, and *Loverine* by Charlotte Meltzer.[43] The vote was close—three in favor to two against in the case of the Gauguin and Henri, with Logan casting a dissenting vote all three times—but it was decided that the paintings would remain. It would not be long, however, before these works would come under fire once more.

At 3:00 that afternoon, the exhibition opened to Art Institute members, along with an exhibition of paintings by Pauline Palmer, whom French had been unable to dissuade from exhibiting with the modernists, and the annual exhibition of American watercolors.[44] Pach, Kuhn, Gregg, and Chanler were joined by American sculptor Jo Davidson, who had only one work in the show but was in town for an exhibition of thirty-five of his pieces at the Reinhardt Gallery. Together they did their best to explain the art to the bewildered public. Carpenter, in a letter to Hutchinson the following day, stated that the exhibition opened "in the finest kind of shape":

> Mr. Aldis, Mr. Eddy and myself were talking the matter over last night and all agreed that the exhibition looked very much better in Chicago than it did in New York. There were about 1500 at the afternoon reception and 302 in during the evening. I have never seen so many automobiles at the Art Institute as there were yesterday afternoon and evening. It seemed that every one of our best citizens who were in town were all here. . . .Mr. Kuhn, Secretary of the Association, and a number of others say they think that our exhibition looks better and is better as a whole than the New York exhibition.[45]

Charles H. Burkholder, French's secretary, while not as enthusiastic as Carpenter, seemed somewhat amused by the events of the first few days of the exhibition as he related them in a letter to the director:

> The hungry crowds are surely upon us. . . .The cubist room, which some have called the Cuban room and the "cubist," referring to the baseball league, was so crowded yesterday that the faces of the visitors were almost against the pictures. In room 50 yesterday, I heard a man laugh at the top of his voice. He inflamed the entire company, and everybody roared. Even Pach, who was with me, became convulsed. The Art Institute is certainly being advertised, but whether to advantage or not, is a question.

Burkholder also reported that the lectures given in the museum's Fullerton Hall by Eddy and Charles Francis Browne, President of the Society of Western Artists and former instructor at the School of the Art Institute, were filled to capacity, with hundreds being turned away. According to Burkholder, "the public wants to hear the 'for and against' or the 'why of art.'"[46]

In contrast to these reports coming from the Art Institute's staff, Kuhn's letters back to New York reveal a different picture. Writing to Elmer MacRae, treasurer of the Association, about the opening day, Kuhn stated:

> Last night was the opening reception, they charged a dollar a head admission to come in and see the "circus" as they call it. We were delicately informed that our presence was not positively necessary. . .but truthfully speaking we were not sorry. They did root up poor Pach about 10 P.M. to have him give a lecture. By the way, all the artistic lights in town are lecturing on Cubism.
>
> The entire situation is different from N.Y. So far the best man is still Aldis, his motives are unselfish. Carpenter has turned out O.K. too, but Eddy has been a source of annoyance. It's a lucky thing that we insisted on our preface to the catalogue otherwise this Chicago bunch would have claimed it all. It was only by strong team work. . .that we prevented all kinds of cheap deals.[47]

Kuhn did not state exactly how Eddy was causing trouble, but no doubt he was busy making a name for himself as Chicago's resident authority on modern art. What probably annoyed Kuhn most was the fact that Eddy seemed more interested in promoting himself than in explaining the new art to the public. In reviewing

FIGURE 18. Cover of the exhibition catalogue for the International Exhibition at the Art Institute. The pine-tree emblem of the Association of American Painters and Sculptors was adapted by Walt Kuhn from a flag used during the American Revolution. This emblem signified what Kuhn called the "new spirit"—that is, revolution—reflected in the modern art in the exhibition.

International Exhibition of Modern Art

Association of American Painters and Sculptors, Inc.

The Art Institute of Chicago

March Twenty-fourth to April Sixteenth
Nineteen Hundred and Thirteen

Eddy's lecture, entitled "The Cubists," the *Chicago Examiner* stated that, "Mr. Eddy shied from the fatal moment of dealing seriously with Cubism, and indulged in many moments of delightful persiflage. . .before he descended to the humdrum task of giving facts and imparting knowledge." According to the newspaper accounts, Eddy at times sounded more like a promoter of investments than of modern art:

> The trouble with most persons, and particularly museums, is that they are about thirty years behind the times: Any of these Cubist pictures can be bought today, while the artists are starving for a few dollars. In thirty years they will be immensely valuable. The Metropolitan Museum in New York bought a Cézanne the other day for $8,000 that it could have had years ago for $150. When the entire world moves up to the value of a new school, then museums and collectors have to pay thirty [times the price].[48]

Eddy's own purchases from the show were noted in most of the newspapers; a few even erroneously reported that he had acquired Marcel Duchamp's *Nude Descending a Staircase,* the most commented upon work in the exhibition. Eddy, however, did claim to have found the actual nude figure in the painting and his diagram, indicating its exact location, was printed in the *Chicago Daily Tribune.*[49] On March 29, Kuhn told Davies that "Eddy had changed his tune," and that he was "endorsing the Association and asking fair play for the exhibitors."[50] In a repeat performance of his lecture on April 3, however, it was reported that Eddy was still congratulating himself for his astute purchases.[51]

While Eddy seems to have squandered his opportunities to defend the modernists, Browne succeeded in disparaging them. In an article under the seditious headline "Chicago Artist Starts Revolt," the *Chicago Daily Tribune* quoted excerpts from Browne's speech in which he related pathological details from the lives of van Gogh and Gauguin, and in a tactic commonly used to dismiss modern art, equated Matisse's art to that of a child's:

> It is related of him [Matisse] that one day he left an unfinished canvas on his easel while he went to lunch. His child wandered in, took some brushes and painted haphazardly and daubed away. Was the child punished? No. Matisse surveyed the work, and exclaimed, "That's it!" and a new school of art was founded.[52]

Kuhn, discouraged by incidents such as these and the way the press covered them, informed his wife that, "the so called intelligent class here are a lot of self advertisers and ignoramuses. Gregg and I are pretty well hated by one or two of them. . . .There were a lot of funny newspaper stories in the papers today. They print anything you tell 'em."[53] Although a few writers had appealed to the reader to approach the exhibition with an open mind—the *Chicago Evening Post* printed an editorial under the title "Fair Play for Insurgent Art"—Kuhn's assessment was regretfully accurate, as the press seemed to be mostly interested in sensational stories (see fig. 19).[54]

In addition to printing comments similar to Browne's, the newspapers were busy providing the public with reams of misinformation. For example, Herman Landon, writing for the *Chicago Record-Herald,* while describing the "seein'-things-at-night vagaries of the ultra-est of the world's Post-Impressionists, Futurists, Cubists, Exceptionists, and all the others," attributed Picasso's *Woman with Mustard Pot* to his dealer, Daniel Henri Kahnweiler, described Brancusi's sculpture *Mlle. Pogany* as a painting, and, without ever having seen the exhibition, discussed the works of the Italian Futurists, who in fact were not included in the show![55] The *Record-Herald* also printed a mock appreciation of the modernists by Otto Nohn Behterr (ought to [have] known better), D.D.S. and Fellow of the Royal Veterinary Society of Honduras, praising the works in the exhibition that depicted animals, and the *Chicago Examiner* ran the headline "Cubist Art Severs Friendships, Institute Directors are Divided" with a reproduction of Marcel Duchamp's *King and Queen Surrounded by Swift Nudes* and a caption stating that the painting was "threatening to cause domestic discord."[56]

The attitude of the Chicago press was probably best summarized by University of Chicago art history professor George B. Zug's assessment in the *Chicago Inter-Ocean:* "As far as real artistic merit is concerned the International Exhibition is the poorest show of equal extent I have ever seen at the Art Institute, yet so far as fun-provoking elements go it beats the record."[57] Discouraged by the paucity of serious and substantive commentary in the Chicago papers, the Association printed a red-covered pamphlet entitled "For and Against" to sell at the Art Institute so that the public might have a chance to be better informed about modern art. Included in the sixty-four page booklet were articles by Gregg and Pach defending the exhibition; a fairly obtuse article, "Cubism by a Cubist," by the artist Francis Picabia; a reprint of a favorable review from the *Chicago Evening Post;* and two reviews criticizing the exhibition, one by noted artist and critic Kenyon

FIGURE 19. Review of the International Exhibition that appeared in the *Chicago Daily Tribune,* March 31, 1913. On the previous day, the exhibition drew a record 18,000 visitors to the Art Institute. The top photograph that accompanies this review shows gallery 53, the "Cubist Room," filled to capacity. See figs. 1 and 14 for other views of gallery 53.

EVANS DESCRIBES DISEASE BATTLE

'Tribune' Health Editor Tells of Prevention Work at Logansport.

RESULTS UP TO PEOPLE.

If Advice Is Followed Physician Believes Fever Epidemic Will Be Averted.

BY DR. W. A. EVANS.

Logansport began on the Wabash and Eel rivers. The narrow valley soon filled with houses and the town extended up the hillside. The railroad tracks, the more important business houses, and many of its people of moderate means remain in the lowlands. Here and there an old family has retained its homestead on an island or at some other desirable place near the river. Generally speaking, the newer houses have been built well above the flood line, for Logansport has had floods before.

The city gets its water supply from the Eel river. It is pumped directly into the mains without filtration or sedimentation.

The people well up the hillside use water from individual wells. These are of the artesian type. The city water is used generally in the lower parts of the town, though in the flats are many dug wells.

Floods Where Danger Lies.

On Monday night the flood rushed down the Wabash and over the low banks into the city streets. Just that part of the city where the flooding was worst was the portion where the water supply could be most polluted by flood water. The yard vaults were washed of their contents, and the washings carried over and into the open wells. The alternative, and the better one at that, was the city water, but it is soupy thick with the turbid flooding of Eel river.

At its worst the water stood ten feet or deeper in the stores and homes. It smeared mud over everything and flowing away left the floors, the streets, whatever it stood over, coated with slimy mud from one inch to three feet thick.

Only two lives were lost by drowning. The loss from wrecked houses and water soaked, mud ruined goods will mount into the hundreds of thousands.

Forced to Drink Polluted Water.

Now comes the aftermath. Since last Tuesday the people have been drinking polluted water.

The water consumed at the flood height was muddy and dirty and bad enough, but it was not as dangerous as is the less muddy but more polluted water now in the mains and wells.

The people are anxious to get Logansport clean. On Saturday morning the streets were being flushed, the cellars pumped out, the floors scraped and washed, and the carpets and rugs sunned and aired. The fight against visible dirt was very much in evidence.

The pollution on the floor may look bad, but the floor is a pretty good place, as places go, for pollution. The pollution that hurts is the pollution that gets in one.

Realizing this, the Logansport authorities commenced getting ready to chlorinate the city water supply. This was to be kept up until all the polluted water had gotten out of the pipes—say for a month.

Peru Needs Cash Aid.

Peru, Ind., March 30.—[Special.]—Mayor John Kreutzer has been besieged with telegrams from many cities asking what outside help is needed most by flood sufferers of Peru. Mayor Kreutzer tonight said:

"The general relief committee and myself have just completed an inspection of the flooded district and we found conditions much worse than we anticipated. The flood sufferers are working diligently to clean up their homes and are aiding in every way to help the relief committee to put the city in a sanitary condition. These people who have been so unfortunate are going to be in need of help in readjusting their homes. Money is needed most of all. Contributions may be sent to Joseph H. Shirk, who is in charge of the finance work."

No additional reports of dead received today and only eight are known to be lost.

Find Four Bodies at Fort Wayne.

Fort Wayne, Ind., March 30.—[Special.]—Bodies of four drowned were found here today. One man was identified by letters from his sweetheart, Viola Adams of Elkhart.

RAILROADS RESUME SERVICE TO THE FLOODED DISTRICTS.

Lines Dispatch Trains from Chicago, Pennsylvania and the Big Four Leading the Way.

An attempt was made by the railroads in Chicago with routes through the flooded district to run trains on the old schedules last night. Several trains left Chicago for cities which have been cut off since the beginning of the flood. It is believed the old schedule will be resumed within a week.

A train for Dayton over the Pennsylvania left the Union station at 11:45 last night. The train will go to Columbus and then to Dayton. It was the first train for Dayton from Chicago since the flood. The Pennsylvania also had a train leaving for Cincinnati at 9:50 o'clock. The Cincinnati train will go by way of Louisville.

The Big Four route has resumed the former schedule from Chicago to Indianapolis. The trains can run no further than Indianapolis. A train left for Indianapolis at 11:55 last night. A train on the Illinois Central for Louisville left at 8:50. The train will go by way of Paducah. It is believed the regular schedule for trains running to the south will be resumed in a few days.

WEAK TRACKS DERAIL TRAIN.

Buffalo Express on New York Central Goes Into Mohawk River, Near Fonda, N. Y.—No Casualties.

Fonda, N. Y., March 30.—Train No. 30, known as the Buffalo express, on the New York Central railroad, was derailed three miles west of here early this morning. Eight cars, including five Pullmans, a buffet car, a day coach, and an express car, were partly submerged in the Mohawk river. The engine, forward car, and two rear coaches remained on the track.

Only seven passengers were slightly injured. Physicians rushed to the scene, attended the injured, and all passengers were transferred to another train and proceeded to New York.

The derailment was due to the undermining of the track embankment by the waters of the Mohawk which have been at flood tide for several days.

Three Identify Purse Snatcher.

Walter Cusick of 711 North Center avenue, was arrested last night and a short time later was identified by three women as the man who snatched their pocketbooks during the last month. Cusick is being held at the West Chicago avenue station.

"Cubist" Photograph of Cubist Crowd at Cubist Exhibit.

Crowds Leaving Art Institute

DRAW LESSONS FROM FLOODS

Chicago Pastors Preach on Ohio and Indiana Calamities.

FAULT OF MEN, NOT GOD.

Declare Lives Not Safeguarded by Public Officials.

Lessons drawn from the recent floods were emphasized in many Chicago pulpits yesterday. It is probable that references of some kind were made in nearly every local church. Prayer for those who had been bereaved of friends or had suffered property loss was a universal petition. In many instances collections were taken for the relief of the flood sufferers.

"It was not God who brought the destruction of the floods but the carelessness of men," said the Rev. F. L. Hayes in his sermon in the California Avenue Congregational.

"The lack of the proper building of bridges, the insufficiency of protection in the making of reservoirs, the indifferent inspection are the responsible causes. The law of the flood must be met by the law of the high ground.

Should Place Responsibility.

"Inspectors ought to be made public officials so that they may be brought under the scope of the law. This ought to be done in Chicago and everywhere so that responsibility can be properly placed. It is the love of God that gives us the fire and the water to be our servants, but as masters they become tyrants. These great losses have brought out much of human sympathy and heroism."

"God never hurt anybody in the whole history of the world just to show that he is great," said the Rev. Frederick E. Hopkins in the Park Manor Congregational church.

"The doctrine that God hated Nebraska, Ohio, and Indiana with such a hatred that he could find no way to satisfy it except by such a calamity would make more infidels than have ever been made in one week since man began to believe anything."

Asks How They Occur.

"How can gigantic calamities occur in a world governed by a good God?" was the subject of the sermon preached by the Rev. Floyd I. Beckwith in the Tabernacle Baptist church.

"Without disaster the world forgets God," said the Rev. Johnstone Myers in his sermon in the Immanuel Baptist church.

Lessons of contentment, gratitude, benevolence, and heroism were drawn from the flood by the Rev. J. P. Brushingham of the South Park Methodist Episcopal church.

JOLIET IN FEAR OF FLOOD.

New Retaining Walls for Sanitary Canal Wanted—Present Banks Said to Be Insecure.

Joliet, Ill., March 30.—[Special.]—Fearing a flood in Joliet unless safety measures are taken, two Joliet papers and the Commercial club are agitating the necessity of new retaining walls for the sanitary canal, together with a butterfly dam in Chicago.

State Representative McCabe and a special committee today investigated, and reported danger at the power plant, two miles north of Joliet. At this point the canal is thirty feet above the surrounding land, and is held by crumbling concrete and dirt banks.

If the walls should give way nothing could stop Lake Michigan coming down.

APOLLO CLUB REHEARSES FOR BIG FLOOD CONCERT.

Disclose Plans Which Promise Successful Musical Entertainment—Proceeds to "Tribune" Fund.

A few outsiders heard the first orchestra rehearsal of the "Damnation of Faust" at the Auditorium theater yesterday afternoon. The Apollo Musical club will give the oratorio next Monday night, April 7, in the Auditorium, as a gigantic benefit for the thousands in Ohio and Indiana who lost their homes in the floods.

The proceeds will be turned over to THE TRIBUNE fund which is being raised for the work of the American Red Cross association at the scene of the floods. The concert is being held under the auspices of THE TRIBUNE.

The rehearsal indicated the concert would win great popular appreciation. The Apollo club is being accompanied by the entire Chicago Symphony orchestra. The music covers a wide range, shifting from pastoral to military, from drinking songs to the Easter hymn.

The scene in Marguerite's chamber was exceptionally good. It suggests the garden scene in Gounod's opera. Marguerite's song is interrupted by the eerie minuet of the will-o'-the-wisps, and this again by the serenade of Mephistopheles with its weird choral accompaniment and bursts of elfish laughter.

Another strong part is the passionate trio in which Faust declares his love, Marguerite accepts it, and Mephistopheles mocks them with a strain that is taken up and expanded by the chorus.

The solo parts are taken by Mme. Mabel Sharp Herdien, soprano; George Harris Jr., tenor; Leon Rains, the Dresden bass-baritone, and Herbert Miller, baritone.

Tickets are selling at THE TRIBUNE office and at the Apollo club office at Lyon & Healy's.

BEATEN BY CAR MEN; MAY DIE

Victim Tries to Halt Kidnaping of Injured Man.

CROWD THREATENS CREW.

Police Arrival Saves Assailants from Rough Handling.

Peter Nielowoczycki of 5116 Lincoln avenue was probably fatally beaten last night by street car employés after he had gone to the assistance of his cousin, Michael Slinger of 5115 Lincoln avenue, who was struck and knocked down by a Lincoln avenue car in front of their home.

Nielowoczycki was taken to the Ravenswood hospital, where it was said that he suffered a skull fracture, three fractured ribs, several knife wounds, and a dislocated shoulder. He told the police that he tried to interpose when the car crew tried to put his cousin on the car to take him to the Sheridan Park hospital.

The car crew, J. R. Fisher, motorman, and C. E. Brigman, conductor, were arrested. Vincent Rouvenek of 1168 North Western avenue and James Rouvinek of 2327 Osgood street, car men not on duty, were also arrested. Police arrived in time to save the car men from a beating at the hands of a crowd which had surrounded the car and was threatening the crew.

NEW YORKER ROBBED OF $80; RECOVERS FUNDS; ARRESTED

Thomas J. Crowley Tells Copper He Won't Prosecute Thief—Policeman Promptly Pinches Him.

In his haste to make a successful "getaway," William Alm sprinted away from his pursuer in Dearborn street last night, and, turning to see if he was followed, ran full into a mail box. The blow knocked his breath from him and Patrolman Michael Hurley got him.

Alm, who says he lives at 3044 Sullivan street, and John Matthews, 2027 Farrell street, are said by Thomas J. Crowley, a New York traveling man, to have seen him display a roll of bills in Stillson's café and snatched $80 from his pocket when they got outside.

Crowley said he had his money back and would not prosecute.

So Crowley was taken along in the wagon, charged with disorderly conduct.

SUNDAY CROWDS SEE CUBIST ART

Record Throngs at Institute Gape at Post Impressionists' Work.

FEW UNDERSTAND THEM.

More than 18,000 Pass Before Weird Productions of Futurists.

More than 18,000 persons yielded to an overwhelming curiosity to see "cubist art as the cubist makes 'em," and thronged the Art institute all day yesterday.

It was a record day for a special art attraction. There have been larger attendances only at times when the crowds were attracted by tournaments in Grant park. The average citizen does not clearly understand what cubist art is, judging from the comment made by visitors who viewed the weird works of the futurists.

"Dear, will you please tell me where the human figure is in this picture with such a shocking title?" asked a prim little woman. She was looking at "Nude Descending a Staircase."

How to Get the Cubist Idea.

"Of course," responded her companion, "you are not supposed actually to see what the artist does. Perhaps it would not be exactly delicate. There is a formula by which you can see just what is represented. Take a careful survey of the picture, study the purported idea, whirl around three times, close your eyes, count twenty, bump your head twice against the wall, and if you bump hard enough the picture of the nude descending the staircase will be perfectly obvious."

Makes Girl Dizzy.

A crowd stood before the "Dance at the Spring," by Francis Picabia. A woman and her little daughter studied the picture seriously.

"How many people can you see in the picture?" asked the mother.

"I think I can see one, mother," the girl replied. "Is it a puzzle picture?"

"No, it is supposed to show the dancer dancing. But where is the figure that you see?" asked the mother.

"It's gone. I can't see it now," answered the girl in astonishment. "O mother, take me away. I feel dizzy. My head is swimming."

"Sheriff Bob" W. Chanler of New York, whose romance with the operatic artist, Cavalieri, made him no less famous than his experience as an officer of the law and an artist, is the most conspicuous exhibiter at the entrance to the cubists' rooms.

WILSON UNLIKELY TO PARDON CASH REGISTER TRUST'S HEAD.

Patterson's Heroic Aid of Flood Sufferers Will Not Relieve Him from Penalty Imposed by Court.

Washington, D. C., March 30.—[Special.]—It is highly improbable that President Wilson will respond to the appeal of Ohio flood sufferers to pardon John H. Patterson, president of the National Cash Register company, who two weeks ago was convicted and sentenced to imprisonment for violating the Sherman anti-trust law.

The fact that Patterson performed splendid service in alleviating the distress of the people of the Miami valley undoubtedly will be of service to him in securing a parole. But a parole cannot be granted until he has served a third of his sentence.

So far as the administration is concerned, it is not willing to pardon a man convicted of such flagrant violation of law as was Patterson. The effort for years has been to secure the imposition of a jail sentence upon a man guilty of trust methods.

$8 YOUR FORM $8
—FOR ONLY
Why Stand for Dress Fittings?
Make Your Own Clothes
On a Duplex Individual Dress Form, modeled according to an impression of your own figure.
Mounted on a standard to your exact height and poise, it eliminates tiresome fittings and makes home dressmaking easy.
Full particulars on application.
Duplex Dress Form Co.
(NOT INC.)
Harrison 3216 Automatic 61455
1100 Republic Bldg., State and Adams Sts.

A Mark-Down Sale of All the Fine Hats at
MAISON PARISIENNE
526 S. Michigan Avenue, Congress Hotel
Beautiful imported Paris Hats that were delayed en route and received too late for the Easter Opening—also exquisite Maison Parisienne Hats, rivaling the Paris creations—all must be sold to make room for the Midsummer Opening and Display. The reduced prices are
$12 $14 $16 $18
Including Numidi and Paradise trimmed and other rare and individual conceptions. SALE BEGINS TODAY.

LADIES AND GENTLEMEN
can now secure "EASE ALL" Shoes at our new loop shop. Here we have a complete stock—all sizes, styles and leathers in
"EASE ALL" SHOES with Built-in Leather Arch Supports
Disarranged arches and varied foot troubles result from wearing shoes that do not fit originally or lose their shape and spread when worn.
"EASE ALL" Shoes provide that "at home" feeling for your feet. The LEATHER arch support permits a natural, springy step, not possible when tramping on METAL BRACES.
Women's $6 "Ease All" Shoes Men's $7
Willis & Atwood Shoe Specialists
Goddard Bldg. Third Floor 27 E. Monroe St. At Wabash Ave.

A. STARR BEST
MADISON AND WABASH
Shepherd Check Spring Coats
With Hats to Match For The Children

Button-to-Neck Reefer
Ages 1 to 4 years
$6.50
Hat to Match, $1.00
Made of fine quality brown and white shepherd check, with embroidered emblem on sleeve, neatly lined throughout, smoked pearl buttons to match.

Notched Collar Reefer
Ages 1 to 8 years
$6.75
Hat to Match, $1.00
Made of fine quality black and white shepherd check, with emblem on sleeve, beautifully embroidered in red and black. Black velvet collar. Carefully lined throughout. Black buttons.
A. STARR BEST
MADISON AND WABASH
CHICAGO

Larson's Anatomic Sta-Right Shoes Correct Broken Arches, Weak Ankles and Flat Feet
STA-RIGHT
Trade Mark Registered
These wonderful shoes are made over your own feet by a plaster paris cast system of shoe building with reinforcements designed especially for each individual's feet.
Made to Measure, $12 and up.
With Plaster Cast, $15 and up.
MARTIN LARSON
Expert Shoe Specialist
369 W. Madison Street At the Bridge.

FIGURE 20. Manierre Dawson (American, 1887–1969). *Helen Darrow,* 1911. Oil on panel; 81 x 59.4 cm. The Art Institute of Chicago, Gift of Manierre Dawson (1968.99). Having developed his own style of abstract painting with little knowledge of the avant-garde movements in Europe, the young Chicago artist Manierre Dawson felt a profound sense of affirmation upon seeing the modern art on display at the International Exhibition in Chicago. While Dawson's portrait of Helen Darrow, the sister-in-law of the lawyer Clarence Darrow, was not included in the International Exhibition, it is representative of the artist's style around the time of the show.

Cox and the other by Princeton art historian Frank Jewett Mather.

The newspaper stories took on a different tone when the commentary moved from the derision of modernist forms to the debate over moral content. On March 27, the *Chicago Record-Herald* reported that a Chicago high school art instructor, after having viewed the exhibition, intended to petition the Board of Education to ban all school children from the exhibition in order to protect them from the "lewd and demoralizing" art.[58] The three works singled out as the worst offenders were the paintings by Gauguin and Meltzer that had come under attack by the museum's trustees, as well as *Models* by Georges Seurat. In an effort to control the damage—and probably also for the sake of entertainment in the midst of all the insanity—Kuhn and Gregg, under the guise of defending the reputation of artist Charlotte Meltzer, contacted the editor of the *Record-Herald,* demanding that he print a retraction by the teacher.[59]

Matters worsened when the Illinois Senate Vice Commission, after hearing of the various criticisms of the International Exhibition, chose to involve itself. M. Blair Coan, charged by the commission to investigate the exhibition, reported, "that he found 'every girl in Chicago' gazing at the examples of 'distorted art' and described *Luxury* by Matisse as a 'distorted female form, with four toes on each foot.'"[60] On hearing Coan's report, at least two senators stated they would visit the exhibition, and letters to the editor appeared in the Chicago papers, condemning the Art Institute for housing such obscenities. The Art Institute eventually forced the Association to withdraw from sale a pamphlet entitled "Noa-Noa," comprised of excerpts from Gauguin's journals, on the grounds that the text was immoral.

Adding to the spectacle of the International Exhibition was the Horticultural Society of Chicago's annual spring flower show at the Art Institute. This exhibit opened on April 1, and included, interspersed among the galleries, all types of plants and aquariums full of rare fish, courtesy of the Chicago Fish Fanciers Club. The combination of the International Exhibition and the flower show was definitely drawing crowds. Burkholder informed French that "everyone in town seems to be headed towards the Art Institute. The attendance on free days runs from 13,000 to 18,000 'souls.'" Burkholder also added that the Horticultural Society had wanted to use Gallery 50, occupied by the International Exhibition, but feared that "the pictures would kill the flowers," and practically every newspaper review of the flower show delighted in repeating similar anecdotes.[61]

Not all Chicagoans who visited the International Exhibition, however, ridiculed it or were opposed to the art displayed. Letters praising the Art Institute for presenting the new art were printed in the newspapers, and even Mayor Harrison claimed that the efforts and explanations of Eddy, Kuhn, and Pach had "made a modernist" of him.[62] But it was on certain members of Chicago's art community that the International Exhibition had its greatest impact.

The author Sherwood Anderson and his brother Karl, a painter who had one of his works in the show, visited the exhibition every day and were inspired by what they saw.[63] Floyd Dell, a writer and editor of the *Friday Literary Review* in the *Chicago Evening Post,* wrote a short story, "The Portrait of Murray Swift," for which he used the International Exhibition at the Art Institute as the setting.[64] The painter Raymond Jonson and the graphic designer E. McKnight Kauffer both spent time at the exhibition and stated that they were greatly influenced by the art they encountered.[65] But the Chicago artist who undoubtedly benefited the most from the International Exhibition was Manierre Dawson.

As early as 1909, Dawson, an architectural draftsman, had been experimenting with abstract painting, unaware of the modern movements abroad (see fig. 20).[66] In 1910, Dawson traveled to Europe, where he learned more about the Post-Impressionists and the modernists and sold one of his paintings to Gertrude Stein, his first sale ever. On returning to the United States, Dawson spent some time in New York and visited Davies in his studio. Davies remembered Dawson when the American section of the International Exhibition was being formed and invited him to participate, but the Chicagoan felt that none of the works he had on hand were ready to show, and did not send any works to New York.

Dawson visited the International Exhibition numerous times at the Art Institute and recorded the events surrounding the exhibition in a journal. After his first viewing of the International Exhibition, Dawson wrote on March 25: "It was with great difficulty that on coming out I could convince myself that I hadn't been through a dream."[67] Pach, noticing Dawson lingering in the galleries, engaged him in conversation and then recognized Dawson as the Chicago artist that Davies had asked Pach to contact. Dawson invited Pach to his home, where he saw Dawson's paintings and took an immediate interest in them.

In his journal entry for March 27, Dawson, while noting the significance of the International Exhibition, expressed regret over the needless commotion that it had caused:

> I go to the Art Institute every day. This is the most important exhibition ever presented in Chicago. It is having terrific impact on the public. The turnstile count has never been so great. . . .The Chicago newspapers are putting out the strangest headings and the silliest comments. The articles in the newspapers sound far more crazy than are the pictures which they are shouting about. "Crazy-quilt," "lumber factory," "nasty," "lewd," "indecent," are the common descriptions. Such terrible misunderstanding when to me, there isn't an insincere work shown. . . .These are without question the most exciting days of my life.

Elated to see that his own artistic experiments were not unlike those of many of the painters represented in the International Exhibition, he wrote that, "I had thought of myself as an anomaly and had to defend myself many times, as not crazy; and here now at the Art Institute many artists are presented showing these very inventive departures from the academies."

Dawson became even more excited when Pach added one of his paintings, *Wharf Under Mountain,* to the American section of the exhibition in gallery 25. Dawson's journal entry of April 4 states:

> Walter [Pach] said he had no trouble getting the painting hung, but if any of the staff should notice it, it might have to come down. He said that so far none of the boss men had come anywhere near the show. I bought every newspaper everyday and searched thoroughly for any mention of the added item. I could find none.

Dawson considered purchasing Picasso's *Woman with Mustard Pot,* but found the price of $675 prohibitive. Instead, on April 7, he purchased a sketch of a nude by Duchamp for $162, and, three days later, bought a painting, *Return from the Chase,* by the Portuguese artist Amadeo de Souza Cardoso, for $54.[68] In his final assessment of the International Exhibition, Dawson stated, "I have learned more from this exhibition than at any previous view of old masters. . . .This exhibition will in all probability have an effect on my painting as well as on thousands of painters throughout the U.S."

Unfortunately, Dawson's enthusiasm was not shared by many Chicago artists. On March 27, the Chicago Society of Artists held a "Futurist Party," lampooning the art in the International Exhibition. The participants came dressed as parodies of the modern painting and sculpture such as "Stewed Descending the Staircase," and "Ace and Ten Spot Surrounded by Nudes." Compositions by Maurice Ravel and Arnold Schoenberg "that everybody said sounded like a nude figure descending a staircase with the force of gravity augmented by the kick from a heavy boot" were played as examples of "Cubist" and "Futurist" music. Said one participant, "We are just showing Cubist and Futurist art as it is. If it is ridiculous, it's not our fault. It is true to the exhibits we have seen."[69]

On April 2, the *Chicago Examiner* reproduced satiric works from a mock Cubist exhibition that was being held across the street from the Art Institute at the Cliff Dwellers, a prominent Chicago arts club. The *Examiner* reported that, "with two or three exceptions, the Cliff Dwellers are more or less violently opposed to the exhibition," and quoted Earl M. Reed, chairman of the club's art committee, as saying, "the caricatures on our walls show infinitely better line and color composition than the works of the cubists and the rest of them, and there is not one [caricature] there that took twenty minutes to complete."[70] Kuhn viewed this behavior by tradition-bound Chicago artists, who stood to lose if academic art fell out of favor with the public, as an act of self-preservation, stating that these artists were, "worried about their bread and butter."[71]

Particularly troublesome, as far as Kuhn was concerned, was the stance of faculty members of the School of the Art Institute, who were swaying the students' opinions against modern art and the International Exhibition. In a letter to Davies, Kuhn stated that, "all the instructors are mad through, one even went so far as to take a big class of students into the French room and threw a virtual fit condemning Matisse. We three [Kuhn, Pach, and Gregg] stood in the hall and laughed at him. However, I had this stopped and after this the lecturing will be done outside the exhibition rooms."[72]

Although Kuhn was originally optimistic about the prospects for the International Exhibition at the Art Institute, by April 5, he had returned to New York and was relieved to be out of "moral" Chicago. Discouraged by the reaction of the public, press, and most of the city's artists, Kuhn wrote to Pach, still at the Art Institute, that "our whole crowd here feels pretty sore about the way things began 'in the beautiful city of the lake'; it seems like a bad dream to me. The outlook for Boston is most encouraging and I hope that the dessert will make up for the bad middle course of the art banquet we furnished for America."[73]

By this time, the Art Institute staff had apparently had its fill of the International Exhibition as well. Burkholder had sent French installation photographs: "You will get a fine idea of the hanging from these photographs. It is undoubtedly true that 'hanging is too good' for some of these pictures."[74] In a separate letter to French, Bessie Bennett, an assistant in charge of textiles and decorative arts, was equally unkind in her assessment of the exhibition:

> Our freak exhibit departs on date specified. I have reason to suppose that it is not altogether a success as the opposition to it has been quite outspoken, and after the first rush of curious visitors seems now to be falling off most decidedly. The gentlemen who came on here have done more harm than the exhibition, their personalities being most undesirable.

Bennett stated her belief that Hutchinson would not have approved of the events surrounding the International Exhibition and criticized Carpenter's abilities as acting director.[75]

Carpenter, to the contrary, painted a different picture to French, stating that, "nothing is suffering here. That is one of the peculiarities of this Institute. It does not make any difference who goes away, the Institute seems to get along just as well, if not better, without them." Carpenter further reported that he and trustee Frank Logan, who was busy answering letters objecting to the International Exhibition, had decided to turn down the Association's offer to extend the exhibition six more days, and that Pauline Palmer had not suffered from exhibiting with the modernists, realizing $2,500 in sales and receiving two portrait commissions. Carpenter also took credit for creating the Association's "For and Against" pamphlet and claimed to be responsible for organizing the lectures by Browne and Eddy:

> I arranged these lectures as I was afraid that our students might get side-tracked in some way by the exhibition. They [Browne and Eddy] gave them a good talk and I feel that the exhibition will not only do them no harm but on the contrary will get them conversant with the movement, with which they will have nothing to do. Mr. Patten, the former architect of the school board, told me that the architects of the United States had to go through the same experience; that is, they studied the disturbance in architecture which arose in Europe only to repudiate them and go on with their work stronger than ever. He was of the opinion that this exhibition would have the same effect on the artists here.[76]

Indeed, there was no need to worry about the students of the school, for on April 16, the closing day of the

International Exhibition, they gathered outside the museum and demonstrated against the show, leaving no doubt that they had rejected the modernists (see fig. 21). The students held a mock trial of the artist Hennery O'Hair Mattress (Henri Matisse), accusing him, "in the name of pure food laws and the committee of streets and alleys. . .of artistic murder, pictorial arson, total degeneracy of color sense, artistic rapine, criminal abuse of title, and general aesthetic abortion." After finding the artist guilty and condemning him to death, the students, "in freakish garbs of every kind, from gaudy bath robes to paint-smeared aprons," marched in a "Cubist" funeral procession, accompanied by "dime store music—the Streets of Cairo kind."[77] The gathering was prepared to burn an effigy of Matisse, but, at the behest of Pach and Elmer MacRae, who had come from New York to conclude business with the Art Institute, Carpenter interceded, and copies after Matisse's *Luxury, Goldfish and Sculpture,* and *The Blue Nude* were burned instead.

The following day, the *Chicago Evening Post* described the gathering of students as a riotous mob: "Two hundred students of the Art Institute, hating even beyond the point of violence, screamed out such fearful imprecations that even the Michigan Avenue policeman became mildly arrested and more than a thousand persons flocked to the scene." The *Post* also quoted one student who was not only enraged with the modernists but with Carpenter, as well:

> "He has turned the Art Institute into a circus. He has gotten out big posters to advertise this thing, which is not art, while he would not exert himself for a real exhibit. So it was determined to present a public rebuke to Mr. Carpenter in particular and to all cubist art and artists in general."[78]

In response to the protests, Pach, according to a *Chicago-Record Herald* article entitled "Cubist Art Exhibit Ends 'at the Stake,'" "offered the opinion that students who yesterday burlesqued and criticized and satirized would, unless they changed their ideas, spend the remainder of their days 'eating crow.'"[79]

With this demonstration, the Art Institute and the city of Chicago bade an unkind farewell to the International Exhibition of Modern Art. Over the next several days, the exhibition was dismantled, the modern European contingent was sent to Boston for a relatively uneventful showing at the Copley Society, and the remaining art works were shipped back to New York to be returned to either their artists or owners.[80] Carpenter, feeling that the Art Institute had paid more than its fair

FIGURE 21. On April 16, 1913, the closing day of the International Exhibition, students of the School of the Art Institute assembled outside the museum to protest the show. The gathering staged a mock trial of Henri Matisse, and burned copies of three of his paintings.

share of the expenses for the exhibition and that the Copley Society was receiving the show at a bargain rate, made the conclusion of business difficult for MacRae. In stating his grievances to Kuhn, Carpenter still remained congenial, writing that:

We have tried in every way to be very liberal in our business relations with the Association and hope that everything will be satisfactory to it. I feel under great obligation to the Association for making this collection and allowing it to come to Chicago. I say this, notwithstanding the adverse criticism which we have received on account of this exhibition. Our people have never wavered for a moment in the matter of having the exhibition here nor have they regretted it. We believe that what we have done has been for the best.[81]

Although Carpenter's claim that the Art Institute "never wavered for a moment" or regretted having the International Exhibition is untrue, the feeling prevalent among those at the museum was that the Art Institute had done a noble deed in presenting Post-Impressionist and modern art to the public. An article in the April issue of the museum's *Bulletin,* issued while the International Exhibition was still on view, commended the Art Institute for having sponsored the exhibition, even while discrediting the majority of the artists who were included:

Question had been raised in some quarters whether the Art Institute does right in exhibiting the strange works of the cubists and post-impressionists; whether a great museum ought not to adhere to standards and refuse to exhibit what it cannot be supposed to approve.

The policy of the Art Institute, however, has always been liberal, and it has been willing to give a hearing to strange and even heretical doctrines, relying upon the inherent ability of the truth ultimately to prevail.

In the present instance it is well known that the radicals and extremists in art have arrested a great deal of attention in Europe, and there naturally is a lively curiosity in art circles here to see their productions. There is no prospect of their being seen here in any comprehensive way unless the Art Institute exhibits them.

The present exhibition is very diverse. It is safe to say that the artists range all the way from the sincere, and usually eccentric, person who has revolted from conventionalism, and seeks relief in novel modes of expression, to the reckless, and often ignorant, fellow who seeks easy notoriety and hopes to impose upon the public.[82]

After returning to Chicago around April 25, French initially expressed fear that the exhibition would have an adverse effect on Chicago's art students, but he quickly felt comfortable dismissing the exhibition as any sort of threat:

There is this to be said in favor of the exhibition; that the Radicals cannot complain that they have not had a fair chance. We have met them on their own ground, and I see no ill results farther than that some people are shocked that the Art Institute should have tolerated such things.[83]

The Art Institute's *Annual Report* for the year 1912–13 and the July issue of the museum's *Bulletin* also echoed the sentiment that the Art Institute, in a sense of fair play, had provided the modernists with the opportunity to present their arguments, which were soundly rejected by a discerning public. Both publications were happy to state that there was no detrimental effect on the impressionable students of the School of the Art Institute.[84]

Although, with museum hours extended from 9:00 A.M. to 10:00 P.M., the International Exhibition drew 188,650 visitors to the Art Institute during the course of its twenty-four day run, it appears, as reported by the Art Institute's publications, that the show did not effect immediate change in Chicago artists or the viewing public. Countering Pach's enthusiastic comment that "the impression on all classes of the big public of Chicago has been a profound one and that it will continue to grow for many years," was Dawson's sober assessment of the city's art scene in the wake of the International Exhibition.[85] On October 5, 1913, Dawson expressed regret in his journal that very few Chicago artists were

feeling around for something more than academic. However, the Art Institute is still hide-bound and even more so than before the Armory Show. Criticism was so severe. . .that those running the galleries are scared to death. Art stores along Michigan Avenue are dead set against anything resembling Cubism. One of the trustees of the Art Institute who thought of buying a Cézanne was talked out of it by ridicule of the examples shown in the International.

Besides Dawson and Eddy, very few Chicagoans bought art from the International Exhibition, and some of these purchases were made in New York, prior to the exhibition's arrival in Chicago.[86]

Of all Chicagoans, Arthur Jerome Eddy was most visible in patronizing modern art after the International Exhibition had departed. Before the exhibition had even closed, Eddy, having instantly acquired a reputation as a collector of the most extreme art, received requests for the loan of his collection from Midwestern museum officials who were hoping to give their public a chance to see what modernism was all about.[87] Eddy spent the summer of 1913 in Europe, seeking out avant-garde art and artists, and expanded his collection by more than one hundred works, including paintings purchased directly from Wassily Kandinsky in his Munich studio, and a bronze casting of a sculpture he had seen in the International Exhibition, Brancusi's *Sleeping Muse.*

Eddy not only expended his energies and income collecting the new art, but also worked at bringing modern painting and sculpture to the attention of the public. In 1914, he wrote *Cubists and Post-Impressionism,* one of the first books published in America on modern art, in which he explained the latest trends in painting and sculpture and included illustrations of works in his collection, as well as excerpts from his correspondence with modern artists.

It was through the efforts of individual artists and patrons that the exhibition came into being, and it was these very individuals who continued to champion Post-Impressionist and modern art after the exhibition had ended. Besides Eddy, the International Exhibition served as an impetus for modern-art collectors such as Walter and Louise Arensberg (see, in this issue, the essay by Naomi Sawelson-Gorse), Albert Barnes, Katherine Dreier, and John Quinn, among others. And through the efforts of Quinn, attorney for the Association of American Painters and Sculptors, the existing tariff on importing contemporary European art in to the United States was rescinded by Congress in October 1913, spurring a rise in the number of American art galleries dealing in modern art.

Yet in spite of this increased activity among dealers and collectors, most American art museums were still reluctant to display and acquire modern art in the decade following the International Exhibition. The Metropolitan Museum in New York had purchased a landscape by Cézanne from the show, but it did not sponsor its first exhibition of Post-Impressionist art until 1921. During the 1920s, many American museums held their first exhibitions or made their initial purchases of Post-Impressionist and early modern art. It was also in this decade that Katherine Dreier formed the Société Anonyme, a forerunner to The Museum of Modern Art, New York, which itself was not established until 1929.[88]

As for The Art Institute of Chicago, the rate at which it accepted modern art was not much different than that of other American museums. In 1915, Arthur Eddy was able to interest the Art Institute in holding an exhibition of paintings by Albert Bloch, an American member of the Munich Blaue Reiter group. But after Eddy's death in 1920, the museum failed, despite the efforts of Aldis, to pursue actively the acquisition of Eddy's collection of modern art.[89] Finally, in 1931, the Art Institute accessioned twenty-three works, including some pre-twentieth-century objects, from what was once a collection of several hundred works, as the Arthur Jerome Eddy Memorial Collection (see figs. 3, 17, and 22).

In 1920, the Art Institute may not have been ready to accept the degree of modernity represented in Eddy's collection, but it was slowly beginning to acquire works

FIGURE 22. Amadeo de Souza Cardoso (Portuguese, 1887–1918). *The Stronghold,* 1912. Oil on canvas; 92.8 x 61 cm. The Art Institute of Chicago, Arthur Jerome Eddy Memorial Collection (1931.512). This is one of three paintings by Souza Cardoso purchased by Eddy at the International Exhibition while it was in Chicago. All three of these paintings are now part of the Arthur Jerome Eddy Memorial Collection at the Art Institute.

by late nineteenth- and early twentieth-century avant-garde artists. In 1920, the Art Institute purchased Redon's collection of his own graphic work from his widow, a significant acquisition considering the fact that Redon's work was unknown in this country prior to the International Exhibition. During the 1920s, under the directorship of Robert B. Harshe, the museum also acquired, through the gifts of the Joseph Winterbotham Fund and the Helen Birch Bartlett Memorial Collection, significant examples of Post-Impressionist painting, including outstanding works by Cézanne, Gauguin, van Gogh, Seurat, and Toulouse-Lautrec, as well as modern paintings by Braque, Friesz, Matisse, Modigliani, Picasso, and Segonzac.[90]

In his introduction to the catalogue for the 1915 "Exhibition of Modern Paintings by Albert Bloch of Munich," Eddy wrote as follows about the Art Institute:

> Of all the public art galleries of the country the Chicago Art Institute had been the broadest in its views of what it owes the public; it has been the most alert to give the public an opportunity to see the latest developments in art in Europe. . . .The trouble with nearly all the other art museums of this country is that those in charge assert the right to say what the public shall and shall not be permitted to see. . . .In opening its doors to exhibitions such as the International and such as the present one of Bloch's, the Trustees of the Art Institute do so on the theory that its members and the public have the right to see and judge for themselves everything that is new and interesting in art, or—to put it in more practical language—the people of Chicago should not be compelled to go abroad to see the new pictures if it is within the power of the Institute to bring the pictures here.[91]

With these words, Eddy paid tribute to the museum for its role in bringing Post-Impressionist and modern art before the public. Despite The Art Institute of Chicago's initial ambivalence toward modernism and the International Exhibition, it was the only public museum in America to have taken the initiative to host this revolutionary show.

Appendix

The letter from William French to Charles Hutchinson of February 22, 1913, assessing the International Exhibition of Modern Art in New York, is published below for the first time in its entirety. The text of this letter is taken from a transcript that can be found in the Department of Archives at The Art Institute of Chicago.

I have seen the International Exhibition of Modern Art. It consists of paintings, drawings, sculpture and a few objects of decorative art, screens, and porcelains (the last insignificant). It occupies eighteen galleries, formed by partitions in a great armory at Lexington Avenue and 25th St., (about 2100 ft. of linear space) and is well lighted and installed. To my surprise, nine galleries, a full half the space, is [*sic*] occupied by American works, some good, some bad, some extreme, some normal. Hassam, Lie, Borglum, Bellows, and Henri are not unexpected, but just what relation C. H. Davis, Weir, Bessie Potter, Fraser, Ruger Donaho have to this exhibition is not clear. Besides this American half there is another fraction given to radicals of former years,—Delaroche, Courbet, Goya, Corot, Manet, Monet, Degas, Puvis de Chavannes, Renoir—so that considerably less than half the exhibition is of the real foreign modernists, and of these some, like the Irish Hone and the English Conder, are scarcely peculiar enough to appear exceptional in any ordinary exhibition. Another considerable fraction of the works exhibited, if offered by themselves, would not arrest attention by any original or striking characteristics, but would appear simply incompetent, just plain bad; uncertain in drawing, crude and tasteless in color, careless and ignorant in execution. In one or two instances, such as Henri Rousseau of France, the artist has succeeded in imitating the naivete of childhood, but for the most part the works are plainly enough sophisticated and studied for effect.

The fraction of the exhibition comprising the real modernists—the post-impressionists, cubists, pointillists, futurists—six or seven galleries, is eminently satisfactory. Anything more fantastic it would be hard to conceive. Some of the works are mere unmeaning assemblages of forms, with gay color, conveying no idea whatever, but bearing such titles as "Dance" or "Souvenir." A few, more logically, have no titles, but merely numbers. As an appeal to curiosity this part of the show is a decided success. Sculpture does not lend itself to idealism of this class, and the statues are clearly explicable, sometimes good in spirit, but generally exaggerated or distorted.

I went over the exhibition with Mr. Davies, the President of the new Association, and with Mr. Kuhn, the Secretary; and also with Mr. Kenyon Cox and Mr. Frederick Crowninshield. I also met at the exhibition, Blashfield, Chase, Bellows, Redfield, and others. Mr. Davies is a sincere and attractive man, and as a painter an accomplished technician. His works are freakish, but they contain fine passages of color and form, which any critic, however classical, will admire. He is eccentric, but his eccentricities are sanity itself compared with the works of the extremists. He however pointed out, with evident sincerity, in the works of such artists as Matisse beauties which I was unable to see. His associates of course expressed similar appreciations, but I saw in their own work no evidences of competency for criticism. I suspect we have here the representatives of the two classes of radicals. First, a few eccentrics, some of them, like Van Gogh, actually unbalanced and insane, who really believe what they profess and practice; secondly, the imitators, who run all the way from sheer weakness to the most impudent charlatanism. The choice is between madness and humbug. How then should these artists have admirers among reasonable people! In the same way the most irrational religious cults attract followers—Bahaism, Teedism, Theosophy, Mormonism, not to mention more fashionable present-day isms, all have respectable disciples. It is simply unaccountable. We have to give it up! Meanwhile the party that has the majority is by definition the rational one, and may venture to assert itself.

With regard to the desirability of bringing the exhibition to Chicago, my opinion has changed. I at first thought it would be a good thing to satisfy the curiosity of the public, and as I visited the exhibition for the first time I felt a sort of exhilaration in the absurdity of it all. I still think it would be reasonable and right for us to exhibit a single gallery, perhaps fifty examples, of the most extreme works, so that our public may know what they are. But when it comes to bringing a large part of the exhibition here (we could accommodate about one-half), to incurring great expense, to turning the Art Institute upside down, as has scarcely been done except in honor of Saint-Gaudens or the Société Nouvelle, I hesitate. We cannot make a joke of our guests. It becomes a serious matter. As I visited the exhibition repeatedly I became depressed, to think that people could be found to approve methods so subversive of taste, good sense and education; of everything that is simple, pure, and of good report. In this feeling I was confirmed by a conversation with Mr. Wm. M. Chase, whom nobody can call a bigot in art matters. I have scarcely ever seen Mr. Chase so serious on any subject. He pointed out that the inevitable inference for an art student, whose inexperience and sensitiveness to impressions must be fully recognized,—the only inference from the respectful recognition of such work, must be, that education and technical training are wholly unnecessary and useless. The whims of ignorance are just as good as the well considered productions of highly trained persons. In this I find myself in agreement with Mr. Chase.

Matisse's work: If this work were submitted to me without explanation, I should regard it as a joke. It is asserted that he is an accomplished painter. I have never seen anything to show it, and I am of the opinion that if he ever did anything really distinguished it would now be exhibited. I think it probable that Matisse, failing to distinguish himself in regular lines, resorted to this work to attract attention. Certainly the work is without merit. It has no subtlety of line, no sweetness of color, no refinement of sentiment, no beauty of any kind.

Redon's work: This work gives more impression of a sincere but unbalanced mind. It is not without beauty and evidences of training, and yet it is irrational. Some of the flower painting, which is much admired, appears to me poor and ineffectual. Davies' work is somewhat akin to this, but technically better.

John's work: A good deal of the English John's work is exhibited. He is the only one who exhibits good, early academic studies, crayon heads, etc. These are good, without being exceptional. His latest work, figure pictures, are decidedly unacademic, but have no resemblance to the French freak works. They carry simplicity to an extreme, and may be described as imperfect rather than revolutionary.

Van Gogh's work: Not so good as I expected from some prints I have seen. Other people have done the same things better. It is well known that he was violently insane.

Duchamp and Picabia: The wildest of the cubists. Humbugs—not incapable.

Gauguin: Heavy and ugly.

The Nervous Profession: Daniel Catton Rich and The Art Institute of Chicago, 1927–1958

JOHN W. SMITH
Archivist
The Art Institute of Chicago

I think the most difficult part [of being a museum director] is that you are fragmented into all kinds of different parts. If you're interested in art and the object and in scholarship, you get farther and farther away from it. . . .Robert Harshe used to call it the "nervous profession."

DANIEL CATTON RICH, 1970

When the trustees of The Art Institute of Chicago announced their choice of Daniel Catton Rich as Director of Fine Arts on May 12, 1938, the *Chicago American* proclaimed, "Chalk up one more for the young 'uns in Chicago executive positions."[1] Indeed, at thirty-four years of age, Rich was the youngest director ever chosen to head the museum (fig. 1). Rich's predecessor, Robert Harshe, who had died in January of that year, was a highly regarded figure in the art world, although he was occasionally criticized by the Chicago press for his "modernistic" tastes. The selection of Daniel Catton Rich, who was known to be an avid supporter of modern art, was a bold move. Perhaps in anticipation of the public's concern that the Art Institute would be entirely turned over to the avant-garde, Rich assured the press that the "immediate policy of the Art Institute is to continue the plans of Mr. Harshe, and I do not think there will be very much change in the line of exhibitions or acquisitions."[2] Nonetheless, over the next twenty years, Rich and the staff he assembled would have a dramatic effect on the museum. By rethinking and revitalizing the Art Institute's policies toward acquisitions, exhibitions, installations, and educational programs, Rich would succeed in creating not merely a museum of modern art, as some feared, but a truly modern museum.

Daniel Catton Rich was born in South Bend, Indiana, on April 16, 1904.[3] His father, Daniel, was a lawyer, and his mother, Martha, had been a school teacher prior to her marriage. Though his parents had some interest in the arts (Mrs. Rich was an amateur watercolor painter), it was one of Rich's aunts, Bertha Beck, who proved to be his most important family ally. Mrs. Beck was a concert pianist who lived in Chicago, and during his youth Rich spent a great deal of time with her and her husband. She was very interested in the visual arts and often took Rich to the Art Institute. In later life, Rich recalled especially their visit to the International Exhibition of Modern Art in 1913.[4] Better known as the Armory Show, the exhibition impressed Rich more for the throngs of people it attracted than by the art it included. The painting that made the strongest impact on him was Marcel Duchamp's *Nude Descending a Staircase, No. 2,* which he was instrumental in bringing back to Chicago for the Century of Progress exhibition in 1933 and again in 1949 as part of the Louise and Walter Arensberg Collection.[5]

Rich was educated in the South Bend public school system, and it was during his high school years that he developed an interest in writing. Initially, he wrote plays for his high school drama club. In 1922, Rich entered the University of Chicago where, refusing a scholarship in chemistry, he majored instead in English, with the hope of pursuing a career as a writer (fig. 2). Theater once again provided an outlet for his talents, and several of his

FIGURE 1. Daniel Catton Rich, 1939. Rich served as director of The Art Institute of Chicago from 1938 to 1958. During that time, he achieved a new level of professionalism throughout the museum.

plays were produced at the university during his time there. It was also at this period that Rich met his future wife, Bertha Ten Eyck James, a fellow student and poet.

After graduating in 1926, Rich, who had become fluent in French, briefly considered becoming a language teacher. Instead, he enrolled in a one-year graduate course in English and art history at Harvard University, primarily to be near his fiancée, who was a scholarship student at Radcliffe College. Although, at this point, Rich had no plans to enter the museum profession, his choice of Harvard could not have been more auspicious, for at this time the university was becoming known as the preeminent training ground for future museum directors and curators, due principally to the ideas and teaching methods of Paul Sachs.

Paul Sachs had joined the Harvard faculty in 1915 as assistant director of the Fogg Art Museum after a brief, unsatisfying career in his family's banking firm, Goldman Sachs (see fig. 3). In the mid-1920s, he began to teach what became known as "Prof. Sachs's museum course," in which he aimed to give students an insider's view of museum work. Sachs, who knew that many of his students would eventually enter the museum profession, recognized that the role of museum directors and curators was rapidly evolving. Knowledge of art history alone was no longer sufficient to meet new challenges, but had to be enhanced with strong administrative and fundraising skills. The significance of Sachs's teaching can be measured in the fact that, at one time, the directors of The Museum of Modern Art and The Metropolitan Museum of Art in New York, The Art Institute of Chicago, and art museums in Minneapolis, San Francisco, Toledo, and Kansas City were all former students of his.[6] While Rich did not take Sachs's course during his year at Harvard—the professor was on sabbatical that year—he did study with his colleague Edward Forbes and, importantly, came into contact with many of Sachs's students. It was at this time that Rich began to consider a museum career.

Upon completion of his year at Harvard, Rich taught English briefly at the University of Colorado, but was unenthusiastic about a life in academia. He soon learned of an opening at The Art Institute of Chicago for an editor of the monthly *Bulletin.* He applied for the

FIGURE 2. Daniel Catton Rich at the time of his graduation from the University of Chicago, 1926. Photo courtesy of Penelope Jarchow.

FIGURE 3. The faculty of the Fine Arts Department, Harvard University, in the Fogg Art Museum courtyard, 1927. Sitting, left to right: Paul J. Sachs, George H. Chase, Denman W. Ross, Edward W. Forbes, Arthur Pope. Standing, left to right: Meyric R. Rogers (who later served as the Art Institute's Curator of Decorative Arts; see fig. 10), Langdon Warner, George H. Edgell, A. Kingsley Porter, Chandler R. Post, Martin Mower, Kenneth J. Conant. Photo courtesy of the Harvard University Art Museums.

FIGURE 4. Robert B. Harshe at his desk, 1937. Harshe was director of the Art Institute from 1921 to 1938. He was a widely-admired museum director, and he accomplished much toward Chicago's acceptance of modern art. Rich frequently acknowledged the debt he owed Harshe for his early training.

job and, in the fall of 1927, returned to Chicago to take up his new position.

The Art Institute in the mid-1920s was an institution experiencing incredible growth. When Robert Harshe arrived as director in 1921, the museum had, as Chicago critic C. J. Bulliet put it, "congeal[ed] into a smugness that was an outgrowth of the traditions of the World's Columbian art show of 1893."[7] Indeed, the institution still strongly bore the conservative stamp of William M. R. French, who had served as its director from 1883 until his death in 1914. With the aid of sympathetic trustees such as Frederic Bartlett, Robert Allerton, and Arthur Aldis, Harshe set about the task of reinvigorating the museum (see fig. 4). One of his plans was to create a more receptive environment for modern art. In 1922, as a step in that direction, he arranged with the Arts Club of Chicago to hold their exhibitions in the Art Institute's galleries. In this manner, the museum was able to expose its visitors to contemporary art without coming under direct attack for showing work that was often unpopular.[8] It was in the early 1920s that the museum acquired some of its greatest and most enduring masterpieces. In 1922, the Art Institute received the magnificent Potter Palmer Collection of French Impressionist paintings, as well as the Mr. and Mrs. W. W. Kimball Collection of primarily eighteenth-century English painting. A few years later, in 1926, the Art Institute received its gift of late nineteenth- and early twentieth-century masterpieces from trustee Frederic Bartlett. Known as the Helen Birch Bartlett Memorial, the collection included works by Cézanne, Gauguin, Picasso, Toulouse-Lautrec, and van Gogh. But the most notable work was Georges Seurat's *Sunday on La Grande Jatte—1884*.[9] The trustees, reluctant to accept Bartlett's gift, agreed only after enormous pressure from Harshe. It was in this environment, one of tremendous growth but lingering conservatism, that Rich found himself in 1927.

The *Bulletin* of the Art Institute was a monthly publication sent to all museum members. It was conceived in 1907 to apprise members of museum exhibitions, lectures, acquisitions, and other news. As editor of the *Bulletin,* Rich was expected not only to edit articles written by others, but to contribute articles of his own. The first issue of the *Bulletin* under Rich's editorship was published in October 1927, and featured a cover story by him on three fifteenth-century Italian paintings on loan to the museum from Martin A. Ryerson. Over successive issues, Rich wrote about museum objects from every department and period. One issue might find him focusing on paintings by Chicago artists, the next on a gift to the museum of an important canvas by Tintoretto or of a Greek amphora. Regardless of the subject matter, even Rich's earliest writings are distinguished by a clarity and directness that were to become his trademark. During his directorship, Rich insisted that this approach become the house style of all Art Institute publications. In the 1970s, when Rich was asked by an interviewer for his thoughts on writing about art, he stated that he felt most art writing was "terribly ponderous." He continued: "I think it obstructs the relation of the writer to the work of art, and therefore the reader to the work of art." He believed that the art historian must never create "a barrier and a barbed wire fence" between viewer and object.[10]

In less than a year after becoming editor, Rich was asked by Harshe to add to his duties the role of Assistant Curator of Painting and Sculpture, a new position created for him. By 1930, Rich had been promoted to associate curator. He worked closely with Harshe in planning exhibitions and in conducting research on the permanent collection. By today's standards, Rich's rapid ascent to associate curator seems astonishing. While it was due in great part to his keen intelligence and personal ambition, it was also indicative of a general trend in the museum world in the United States in the late 1920s, when people in their late twenties and early thirties were increasingly assuming positions of power. In 1929, the twenty-seven-year-old Alfred H. Barr, Jr., had been hired as the first director of The Museum of Modern Art in New York; and, in 1927, A. Everett "Chick" Austin, who at age twenty-seven had been made director of the Wadsworth Atheneum in Hartford, Connecticut, was attracting attention with his unorthodox acquisitions and avant-garde exhibitions.[11] The taste and opinions of this generation had a revolutionary effect on American art museums. As Rich later stated:

> [We were] trained in the universities of the country where fine arts courses were at last becoming difficult enough to seem respectable, we had travelled and read; we had our preferences which were not those of the preceding epoch; we were bored with Italian Primitives and stirred by the Baroque. . . .We were born into modern art and knew this year's model of Picasso from last year's; we were not afraid of Surrealism and looked down on Monet. . . .We admitted that photography could be art and thought Mies Van Der Rohe's Barcelona Pavilion the greatest piece of architecture since Robie House or possibly Chartres Cathedral.[12]

In light of these comments, it is not all that surprising that Harshe and forward-looking Art Institute trustees recognized the need for input from someone such as Rich.

The first exhibition Rich organized was "Paintings, Pastels, and Drawings by Odilon Redon," held at the Art Institute from December 27, 1928, to January 27, 1929. Among the show's fifty objects were major works from important collectors, such as Lillie Bliss, and from Ari Redon, the artist's son, along with some of the more than two hundred works that the museum had purchased from Redon's widow in 1920. Rich wrote a short essay for the exhibition catalogue that reveals his formidable knowledge of music, literature, art, and history. Given Rich's background in literature and his fluency in French, the literary artist Redon was an ideal subject for the young author's debut exhibition. Although his taste was quite catholic, it was late nineteenth-century French art that continued to inspire some of Rich's most eloquent and insightful writing, as his later monographs on Cézanne, Degas, Rousseau, and Seurat demonstrate.[13]

In the museum's *Annual Report* for 1930, Harshe wrote that, because of the nationwide financial depression, "all institutions dependent on public support have suffered a diminution in income and the Art Institute in particular has suffered severely."[14] Yet, despite the Depression and the necessary cutbacks in programming, the museum continued to add considerably to its collections in the early 1930s, primarily through a series of magnificent bequests. And, in 1933, the Art Institute staged an exhibition that attracted international attention, adding immeasurably to its reputation.

FIGURE 5. Mrs. Chauncey McCormick, Mrs. Joseph Patterson, and Mrs. Lewis Larned Coburn at the opening reception for the exhibition of Mrs. Coburn's collection, 1932. Upon Mrs. Coburn's death the following year, her collection of Impressionist and Post-Impressionist paintings were bequeathed to the Art Institute.

The first major collection acquired during this period was presented in 1931 by the widow and son of Chicago collector Arthur Jerome Eddy. Comprising over twenty works of contemporary painting and sculpture, the collection was particularly notable for its examples of twentieth-century German painting, including several works by Kandinsky. In December 1931, Rich organized an exhibition of the Eddy Collection and wrote the accompanying catalogue.[15] The year 1933 saw the arrival of two more collections of enormous importance to the museum: a group of sixty-nine Impressionist and post-Impressionist paintings and watercolors from Mrs. Lewis Larned Coburn (see fig. 5), and the vast collection of Martin A. Ryerson, which enriched virtually every department of the museum. As was the case with the Eddy Collection, Rich was given the task of cataloguing the works in the Coburn Collection, including masterpieces by Cézanne, Degas, and Renoir. He also mounted an exhibition and prepared a publication to accompany it.[16] While his work on these collections was valuable preparation for Rich's eventual career as director, nothing could compare to the experience he received from his involvement in the Century of Progress Exposition, staged in 1933 and 1934 to celebrate the centennial of Chicago's founding.

FIGURE 6. Rich and author Hervey Allen with Hans Holbein's *A Lady of the Cromwell Family* (c. 1535/40; The Toledo Museum of Art) at the Century of Progress exhibition, 1933.

A Century of Progress

Planning for the Art Institute's role in the Century of Progress Exposition began as early as 1929, when Harshe was sent to Europe by the Fine Arts Committee of the Century of Progress Exposition to try to secure loans from European museum officials. Harshe had hoped to include in these plans an addition to the Art Institute building to house the exhibition, which would later be used to display the museum's permanent collection. However, the financial crash of late 1929 effectively put an end to such elaborate ideas and the budget for the fine-arts component of the Exposition was drastically reduced. The Board of the Exposition then proposed an exhibition that would feature the "Ten Most Beloved Pictures in America," including Jules Breton's *Song of the Lark* (The Art Institute of Chicago), and Rosa Bonheur's *Horse Fair* and Emanuel Leutze's *Washington Crossing the Delaware* (both in The Metropolitan Museum of Art, New York). Realizing that the city of Chicago would be ridiculed in the press if such an exhibition took place, Chauncey McCormick, the chairman of the Fine Arts Committee, fought vigorously to kill this proposal and once again went to Harshe for a solution.

The resulting Century of Progress exhibition, assembled almost entirely from collections in the United States, was, by all accounts, one of the most magnificent ever mounted in this country before or since. In chronological sequence, Harshe displayed over one thousand works to illustrate the history of Western art from the thirteenth-century Italian "primitives" to the most recent of the European and American avant-garde. During its six-month run, the exhibition attracted over 1.5 million viewers. After it closed, Harshe rehung the Art Institute's permanent collection, for the first time, in the same chronological manner—rather than by donor, as it had previously been installed.[17]

Although the exhibition was largely the brainchild of Harshe, Rich played a key role (see fig. 6).[18] Rich's primary contribution to the Century of Progress show was editing the massive exhibition catalogue.[19] It was the most ambitious publishing venture undertaken by the Art Institute up to that time, being not only a checklist of the exhibition, but an extensive examination of the artists represented in the show. The catalogue received wide praise and was hailed as a "milestone in the history of art exhibition catalogues."[20]

Soon after the closing of the Century of Progress exhibition, Rich embarked upon another publishing project. This one, however, rather than featuring works by hundreds of artists, was focused on one painting, *A*

Sunday on La Grande Jatte—1884 by Georges Seurat. The book's purpose was to document as many of Seurat's preliminary studies for his masterpiece as possible and to examine how the process of completing the painting took shape. Rich spent over two years researching *Seurat and the Evolution of "La Grande Jatte,"* corresponding with dozens of scholars and collectors.[21] While Rich's high-modernist viewpoint of Seurat's painting has fallen largely into disfavor—to be replaced by an approach that gives greater consideration to "the social, political, and economical forces operating in the period in which [the artist's] work was produced"[22]—it nonetheless retains its position as the first truly serious study of Seurat's masterpiece, and one of the first books devoted entirely to one artwork.

The death from a heart attack of Robert Harshe in January 1938, at the age of fifty-eight, was a shock to the museum staff and to the art world. Telegrams of condolence poured in from artists, art historians, collectors, and museum directors from around the world, attesting to Harshe's eminence. Many of the messages praised Harshe as the leading museum director of his generation. Jere Abbott, director of the Smith College Art Gallery and formerly associate director of The Museum of Modern Art, wired Rich that, "of all the directors of the older generation we of the younger group felt him always the most sympathetic."[23] The personal loss to Rich was enormous. Joseph Winterbotham, an Art Institute trustee, wrote to Rich from Paris: "I realize how closely and happily you were associated and I think I understand how deeply you must feel his loss."[24] Rich was understandably very distressed over Harshe's death. He later acknowledged that Harshe had been a wonderful teacher and that the tone of their relationship had often seemed like that of a father and son. Immediately after Harshe's death, Rich set about organizing a memorial retrospective exhibition of Harshe's own paintings.[25] A talented amateur painter, Harshe had chosen never to publicly exhibit his works for fear of a possible conflict with his duties as a museum director. To honor the man, Rich assembled a group of eighty-nine paintings that were shown at the Art Institute and subsequently traveled to over a dozen other institutions.

While Rich was organizing the Harshe exhibition, the trustees of the Art Institute were busy choosing Harshe's successor, reportedly amid great conflict.[26] Potter Palmer II, the chairman of the Art Institute Board of Trustees, had been named director pro tem until a replacement could be found (see fig. 7). Although Rich appeared to have been Harshe's heir apparent, there were trustees who felt he was too young and inexperienced for the position. Also, Charles Kelley, who served as assistant director under Harshe, as well as

FIGURE 7. Potter Palmer II, a trustee of the Art Institute from 1920 to 1943, served as the museum's president from 1925 to 1943. He guided the museum through the difficult years of the Depression and was a strong supporter of Rich's directorship.

Curator of Oriental Art, was reportedly very interested in the job and had the support of the more conservative faction of the board. One story told by a former museum staff member, but perhaps apocryphal, describes Kelley moving into Harshe's office the day after his death, under the assumption that the job would be his. If so, it must have been a severe blow to him when, in May, four months after Harshe's death, the board named Rich the new Director of Fine Arts.

In his first report to the Board of Trustees in the *Annual Report* for the year 1938, Rich spelled out the objectives that were to receive his fullest attention over the next few years.[27] The first of these was to strengthen the program of museum education. The second was to assemble a stronger and more competent curatorial staff, as the museum was "still seriously handicapped by the lack of trained museum workers."[28] Rich focused much of his energy over the next few years on meeting these objectives and, by the end of the war, in 1945, he had made impressive strides toward realizing them.

Addressing Education

In a lecture delivered in 1955, Rich stated that museum education should be made the "core, rather than the fringe of a museum program." He added that museum directors and curators must recognize "that the chief function of an educational department is not to sell what the staff had happily dreamed up, but to help judge and consider from the beginning whether such an exhibition or such an installation, or such and such a purchase best serves the educational needs of your museum."[29] At the time when Rich took over, museum education at the Art Institute was divided among three departments: the Department of Education, the Membership and Extension Lecture Department, and the Children's Museum.

Defined as "the interpreter to the public of the collections of the Art Institute," the Department of Education was responsible for tours of the collections, gallery lectures, and general lectures on the history of art.[30] The Extension Lecture Department catered strictly to the Art Institute's membership, and its programs more often than not dealt with topics such as "Art Through Travel" or "The Clinic of Good Taste," which involved demonstrations on home decorating. The Children's Museum featured small exhibitions designed for young visitors. While these programs were very popular, Rich recognized that the museum ought to develop art-education programs in which the public was more directly engaged with looking at art and where art was explained in terms that were more accessible to them. In 1939, Rich reorganized the Children's Museum as the Gallery of Art Interpretation, the "first permanent interpretive space for adults established by an American museum."[31] The Gallery of Art Interpretation was initially administered by Helen Mackenzie. After Mackenzie's retirement in 1943, Rich handed over the gallery to Katharine Kuh, who would eventually create a series of exhibitions in visual education that was admired and copied by museums around the world (see fig. 21).

Another innovation initiated by Rich was a series of symposiums and seminars that were held in conjunction with major exhibitions. The first of these occurred during "The Art of Goya" exhibition in 1941. These gatherings of experts and scholars have over the years become an integral part of museum exhibitions, creating an important forum for the exchange of new information.

In a similar vein, in 1944, Rich, with the cooperation of the University of Chicago, organized a conference at the Art Institute entitled "The Future of the Art Museum as an Educational Institution." Over fifty representatives from twenty-three institutions were present to hear addresses delivered by eighteen of the most prominent men and women active in art history, education, and radio and television. Among the speakers were David Finley, director of the National Gallery of Art; Henry Francis Taylor, director of the Metropolitan Museum; Juliana Force, director of the Whitney Museum of American Art; and Alfred Barr. Rich discussed the important role that special exhibitions played in the museum's programming, and cautioned that they nonetheless should never preempt a museum's commitment to its own collection. The papers from the conference were subsequently published over several issues of *Museum News*.[32]

Early on, Rich learned to exploit the possibilities of mass media as part of the Art Institute's educational programming. He frequently incorporated film programs in conjunction with the exhibitions, often borrowing material from the film library of The Museum of Modern Art. Rich and the curators appeared regularly

FIGURE 8. Rich with his daughter Penelope near their home in Winnetka, Illinois, c. 1940.

FIGURE 9. Frederick Sweet, Curator of Painting and Sculpture at the Art Institute, at left, with William Deknatel, a member of the Society for Contemporary American Art, 1952. Sweet was Rich's first major staff appointment upon becoming director. He remained at the Art Institute until his retirement in 1968, organizing many notable exhibitions, particularly in the field of nineteenth-century American art.

on local radio shows to discuss current museum exhibitions or recent acquisitions. The Art Institute was also among the first museums to recognize the potential of television to reach a larger audience and, as early as 1954, Rich had created a Department of Television to explore this new technology. Although very ambitious plans, which included a television studio on the Art Institute premises, were made for the department, it was not until 1956 that a program was produced by the museum. Entitled "The Christmas Story in Art," it was aired on WTTW, Chicago's educational television channel, on December 19 of that year.[33]

Building a Staff and Building a Collection

Rich admitted that he was unhappy with the staff that he inherited from the previous administration.[34] He considered an institution without a dedicated staff to be merely "a storehouse of dead objects and useless instrumentalities."[35] Within his first year as director, he had begun to make enormous strides in assembling a team of distinguished professionals who would help create new departments and revitalize old ones. While Rich remained in charge of the Department of Painting and Sculpture, he hired Frederick Sweet as his assistant (see fig. 9). Educated at Harvard, Sweet had taken the museum course taught by Paul Sachs, and was director of the Portland Art Museum in Oregon when Rich hired him.

Sweet was largely responsible for the area of American art. In a landmark exhibition of 1945, he helped renew interest in the Hudson River Valley painters with a large show devoted to their work. Over the years, Sweet continued to organize important exhibitions of American artists. In 1966, he published a biography of Mary Cassatt that drew extensively on the Cassatt family papers, most of which had never been published.[36] His book shed much new light on Cassatt and helped to secure her position in American art history.

In 1938, Rich created the Department of Public Relations and placed Lester Bridaham in charge. The idea of such a department was still novel for a cultural institution in 1938, but, with increasing attacks from the museum's conservative critics, Rich recognized the wisdom of having a professional on the staff to help deal with controversial matters. He also hoped that this department would assist in getting less coverage for the Art Institute on the society pages of the newspapers and more as serious news. This, he believed, would change the perception of many Chicagoans that the museum was an elitist organization by projecting a more populist approach.[37]

After the death of Bessie Bennett, Curator of Decorative Arts, in 1939, Rich found an admirable replacement in Meyric Rogers, director of the St. Louis Art Museum (fig. 10). Associated with the Art Institute almost from its beginnings, Miss Bennett had started the Department of Decorative Arts. She was widely admired for her installations, leading Robert Harshe to comment that "Miss Bennett could display a washcloth and make it look like lace, and often did."[38] With Rogers's appointment came the addition of a new division of Industrial Arts, the focus of which was design in industry and mass production. This new concern of the department was undoubtedly inspired by the presence of the Institute of Design in Chicago, whose faculty was composed of many members of the New Bauhaus, including Lazló Mohóly-Nagy. Plans for the Industrial Arts division were slow to get started, but, by the early 1950s, Rogers was organizing important exhibitions on contemporary industrial design and decorative objects created for the mass market. According to Rich, Rogers also weeded out a great deal of inferior material in the Department of Decorative Arts and began to put together a fine collection of American furniture.[39]

The Department of Prints and Drawings had a full-time curator as early as 1922. Nevertheless, the collection had developed in a haphazard manner with no real focus. This was to change when Rich hired Carl O. Schniewind as curator in 1940 (fig. 11). Schniewind had served as Curator of Prints and Drawings and Librarian at the Brooklyn Museum prior to coming to Chicago. With his rigorous European training and highly developed taste, Schniewind built the Art Institute's department into one of the great collections in the United States during his seventeen-year curatorship. Although he placed particular emphasis on acquiring French prints and drawings of the seventeenth to nineteenth centuries, mirroring the strengths of the museum's painting collection, his inter-

FIGURE 10. Meyric Rogers, whom Rich hired as Curator of Decorative Arts in 1939. Rich had known Rogers during his student days at Harvard University, where Rogers had been on the faculty of the Fine Arts Department (see fig. 3). One of Rogers's main interests was American decorative arts, and he greatly improved this area of the museum's collection.

FIGURE 11. Carl O. Schniewind, Curator of Prints and Drawings, 1957. Rich brought Schniewind to Chicago from the Brooklyn Museum, where he served as Curator of Prints and Drawings and Librarian. Educated in Europe, Schniewind began collecting prints during his youth. To the Art Institute's Department of Prints and Drawings he brought an unparalleled level of professionalism and connoisseurship. By the time of his death in 1957, the Art Institute's collection of prints and drawings was one of the finest in the United States.

FIGURE 12. Katharine Kuh, 1953. Kuh began her sixteen-year tenure at the Art Institute in 1943 as a war-time replacement for the head of the Department of Public Relations. She was soon assigned control of the Gallery of Art Interpretation, where she mounted innovative exhibitions intended to deepen the public's understanding of art (see fig. 21). Eventually, she became the museum's first Curator of Modern Painting and Sculpture, and she acquired many of the museum's key works of twentieth-century art.

ests also ranged much wider. He oversaw important purchases of photography and modern prints and drawings, and staged many exhibitions of contemporary artists. His assistant, Hugh Edwards, played a key role in assembling the museum's collection of photographic works.

Rich's next major staff appointment came about as a result of the United States' involvement in World War II. In 1943, Rich hired Katharine Kuh as Public Relations Counsel (fig. 12) to temporarily replace Lester Bridaham, who had entered military service. From 1935 until 1942, Kuh had operated the Katharine Kuh Gallery, the first commercial gallery in Chicago to show avant-garde European and American art. The gallery also exhibited "primitive" art, photography, and typographical design as art forms. It quickly became apparent that Rich had found in Kuh a kindred spirit who shared his views on the importance of education. After assuming the position of Curator of the Gallery of Art Interpretation in late 1943, she was named Associate Curator of Painting and Sculpture in 1948. In this new capacity, Kuh dealt almost exclusively with the museum's growing collection of twentieth-century works. She would eventually become the Art Institute's first Curator of Modern Painting and Sculpture (1954) and helped secure for the museum several of its key twentieth-century works. She also organized important exhibitions of modern art for the museum, including "Abstract and Surrealist American Art" (1947), in collaboration with Frederick Sweet; "Twentieth-Century Art: From the Louise and Walter Arensberg Collection" (1949) (see, in this issue, the essay by Naomi Sawelson-Gorse); and a major exhibition of the art of Fernand Léger (1953). In 1956, she was chosen to organize the United States Pavilion in the Venice Biennale (see fig. 22).[40]

With this team of curators, Rich undertook to reorganize departments and reinstall many of the museum's galleries. He oversaw the expansion of the museum's collecting interests and the formation of the Department of Primitive Art, which is known today as the Department of Africa, Oceania, and the Americas. He continued a process begun under Harshe to modernize the galleries, relieving them of Beaux-Arts details and updating the lighting and environmental conditions. His concern for the physical condition of the museum's collection led him, in 1956, to appoint Louis Pomerantz as the Art Institute's first full-time conservator. Rich and his staff also began to weed the collections of material that they felt did not measure up to the quality they desired for the museum. This led to a controversial series of deaccessions in the mid-1940s, with the profits being used to purchase works to fill in gaps in the collection.[41]

During Rich's directorship, a number of important collections came to the Art Institute both by gift and bequest. The Charles H. and Mary F. S. Worcester Collection, which was especially rich in early German and Italian painting and which Rich had played a key role in forming; the Max Epstein Collection of Old Masters; and the Alfred Stieglitz Collection, with important works by twentieth-century American artists, such as Arthur Dove, John Marin, and Georgia O'Keeffe.

Rich, with the assistance of his curators, also acquired through purchase many important objects for the museum. When asked what he considered to be among his most important acquisitions for the Art Institute, Rich mentioned "a marvelous late Turner; one of the great Magnascos of the world; a wonderful Matisse mural which we got through trade of a Toulouse-Lautrec, a wonderful picture. A very important Claude Lorrain."[42] The paintings Rich was referring to are Joseph Mallord William Turner's *Valley of Aosta—Snowstorm, Avalanche and Thunderstorm* (1836/37); Alessandro Magnasco's *Synagogue* (1725/35); Henri Matisse's *Bathers by a River* (1909–16; fig. 13); and Claude Lorrain's *View of Delphi with a Procession* (1673; fig. 14).

Rich also purchased important early Spanish paintings such as Juan Sánchez Cotán's *Still Life* (c. 1602; fig. 15) and Francisco de Zurbarán's *Crucifixion* (1627). Particularly fond of Italian painting of the seventeenth century, Rich added several examples during the 1940s, including Bartolomeo Manfredi's *Cupid Chastised* (1605/10) and Guercino's *Entombment of Christ* (c. 1656).

In the field of eighteenth- and nineteenth-century American art, where the Art Institute's collection had been quite weak, Rich oversaw significant acquisitions, including John Singleton Copley's *Mrs. Daniel Hubbard* (1764; fig. 16) and Gilbert Stuart's *Major-General Henry Dearborn* (1812). Other important purchases in this area included William Sidney Mount's *Walking the Line* (1835), Thomas Cole's *Niagara Falls* (1830–31), and Winslow Homer's *Croquet Scene* (1866).

Either by gift or purchase, Rich also acquired a number of major works of twentieth-century art, such as Picasso's *Daniel-Henry Kahnweiler* (1910), de Chirico's *The Philosopher's Conquest* (1914), Orozco's *Zapata* (1926), Hopper's *Nighthawks* (1942; fig. 17), and Sheeler's *Artist Looks at Nature* (1943).

The War Years

When the United States entered World War II in December 1941, the Art Institute mobilized quickly to assist. Rich and the Board of Trustees believed that the institution should play an active role in boosting public morale during the war; to do so, the museum maintained an impressive schedule of programming. Mostly this was in the form of war-related exhibitions, increased lectures, and a series of "Midday Victory Concerts." The museum also opened a Serviceman's Lounge to encourage GI's to visit the museum during their leaves. Many staff members were recruited to work in the war effort, which meant a slowdown in some areas of the museum,

FIGURE 13. Henri Matisse (French, 1869–1954). *Bathers by a River*, 1909–16. Oil on canvas; 261.6 x 391.2 cm. The Art Institute of Chicago, Charles H. and Mary F. S. Worcester Collection (1953.158). This painting and the four that follow (figs. 14–17) are among the many important works that the Art Institute added to its permanent collection while Rich was director.

FIGURE 14. Claude Lorrain (Claude Gellée; French, 1600–1682). *View of Delphi with a Procession,* 1673. Oil on canvas; 101.5 x 127 cm. The Art Institute of Chicago, Robert A. Waller Memorial Fund (1941.1020).

FIGURE 15. Juan Sánchez Cotán (Spanish, 1561–1627). *Still Life,* c. 1602. Oil on canvas; 67.8 x 88.7 cm. The Art Institute of Chicago, Gift of Mr. and Mrs. Leigh B. Block (1955.1203).

FIGURE 16. John Singleton Copley (American, c. 1738–1815). *Mrs. Daniel Hubbard,* 1764. Oil on canvas; 127.6 x 101 cm. The Art Institute of Chicago, Art Institute Purchase Fund (1947.28).

FIGURE 17. Edward Hopper (American, 1882–1967). *Nighthawks,* 1942. Oil on canvas; 84.1 x 152.4 cm. The Art Institute of Chicago, Friends of American Art Collection (1942.51).

FIGURE 18. In 1943, Rich and the Art Institute gave Georgia O'Keeffe her first museum retrospective exhibition. Rich was a great admirer of the artist's work, and they developed a lasting friendship at the time of the exhibition. O'Keeffe's *Black Cross, New Mexico* (1929), which is second from the left in this photograph from the 1943 exhibition, was later purchased by Rich for the museum's permanent collection.

but, overall, the museum not only functioned normally during the war, but was more active than ever.

During the war, communication with the European art world was effectively shut off. This situation had far-reaching implications for the museum because it meant that curators, when planning exhibitions, could no longer count on foreign loans and had to draw almost exclusively from American collections. Despite this handicap, the war years saw a succession of distinguished exhibitions including, in 1941, the exhibition on Goya mentioned above, organized in tandem with The Metropolitan Museum of Art; a major show of the works of Henri Rousseau in 1942 that Rich, who also prepared the catalogue, put together with Alfred Barr and The Museum of Modern Art; and, the same year, an exhibition of seventeenth-century Dutch painting.

The year 1943 was an especially momentous one for Rich and for the Art Institute. In September 1943, Board of Trustees President Potter Palmer II died, and was succeeded by Chauncey McCormick (see fig. 20). McCormick would serve as president until his own death in 1954, and during this period gave Rich his full support. He assured Rich from the beginning that he would "not interfere with the professional side of the museum. We have a staff of experts and we must respect their judgment."[43] McCormick, who had a genuine interest in art, had been involved with the museum for many years. He had come to know Rich especially well during the Century of Progress exhibition, having served as the Chairman of the Fine Arts Committee. He and his wife, Marion McCormick, the daughter of collector Charles Deering, had also enriched the museum's holdings with several works of art, including Martorell's *Saint George Killing the Dragon* (c. 1438) and El Greco's *Saint Martin and the Beggar* (1599/1604).

Another highlight of 1943 was the loan of fifty-two twentieth-century French paintings from the collection of Mr. and Mrs. Chester Dale. A New York stockbroker, Dale began collecting art in the late 1920s and, by the early 1940s, he had formed one of the finest collections of its kind. The Dale Collection was placed on indefinite loan to the museum for nine years, but in 1952 the owners abruptly and rather unceremoniously transferred it from the Art Institute to the National Gallery in Washington, D.C., where Dale was to serve as president of the Board of Trustees from 1955 until 1962. Elected an Art Institute trustee in 1944, he resigned the same year he withdrew his collection. Although they were aware that Dale was being avidly courted for his collection not only by the National Gallery, but by the Philadelphia Museum of Art and several other major institutions, Rich and the trustees, with apparent naivete, assumed the paintings would remain in Chicago. The withdrawal of the collection hit Rich particularly hard, as he had devoted much time to advising Dale on the formation of the collection.[44]

Rich also organized one of the most important exhibitions held during the war years. The "Retrospective Exhibition of Paintings by Georgia O'Keeffe," the first extensive show of O'Keeffe's work at a major museum, opened in January 1943 (see fig. 18). Of all of the contemporary artists whose careers Rich followed and helped to nurture, it was O'Keeffe in whom Rich took the greatest interest. He had first met the artist in Taos, New Mexico, in 1929, at the home of the wealthy bohemian Mabel Dodge Luhan.[45] Luhan dominated the artistic community in Taos, where she was known as the "Empress of Mabel-town."[46] O'Keeffe was visiting New Mexico for the first time, as was Rich. He already knew of O'Keeffe's work from her shows at Alfred Stieglitz's American Place gallery in New York, and he was deeply impressed upon meeting the artist. Rich continued to follow O'Keeffe's career with interest, and when he met her again at a party in New York several years later he suggested that the Art Institute might give her a one-person show. O'Keeffe, who had been a student at the School of the Art Institute in 1905–06, greeted the idea with enthusiasm. Before arrangements for the exhibition could be finalized, however, O'Keeffe and her husband, Alfred Stieglitz, asked the Art Institute to comply with two prerequisites. The first was that the museum would purchase one work from the exhibition, which Rich was happy to agree to (see fig. 18, which includes the painting that the Art Institute chose to acquire: *Black Cross, New Mexico*). The second stipulation was that O'Keeffe be allowed to install the show herself, which she did. The exhibition met with popular and critical success and was an important milestone in O'Keeffe's career. For the catalogue, Rich wrote a highly evocative and poetic essay, which, as a recent O'Keeffe biographer has pointed out, "contained the biographical structure of the O'Keeffe myth as it would be retold again and again."[47]

At this time, Rich and O'Keeffe embarked upon a lasting friendship. In 1945, when she was overseeing the dispersal of the Stieglitz Collection, she relied heavily on Rich's expertise, for which the Art Institute was amply rewarded when O'Keeffe gave a significant part of the collection to the Art Institute.[48] The Art Institute's portion of the Stieglitz Collection includes the core of the museum's earliest group of photographs and a number of important modern paintings, particularly American works.

The Postwar Years

The years following the end of World War II, although not without their problems, can in many ways be considered the golden period of Daniel Catton Rich's directorship. He now had in place a team of gifted curators, as well as a highly supportive president of the Board of Trustees. With their assistance, Rich was able to fill these years with a series of remarkable acquisitions, exhibitions, publications, and educational programs.

Immediately after the war, in 1946, Rich organized an exhibition of British painting that would help define the tone and ambitious scope of Art Institute exhi-

FIGURE 19. Rich with Mrs. Potter Palmer II (left) and Mrs. Tiffany Blake, c. 1950. The two women were important donors to the museum and had a friendly rivalry over their gifts to the Department of Prints and Drawings.

FIGURE 20. Chauncey McCormick, president of the Art Institute from 1943 until his death in 1954; Sir Kenneth Clark, director of the National Gallery, London; and Mrs. Daniel Catton Rich, at the opening of the exhibition "Masterpieces of English Painting: Hogarth, Constable, Turner," October 15, 1946.

FIGURE 21. Installation view of "Constable and Turner: The Road to Impressionism," organized by Katharine Kuh for the Gallery of Art Interpretation in 1946 as part of the exhibition "Masterpieces of English Painting: Hogarth, Constable, Turner." Kuh frequently conceived installations in the Gallery of Art Interpretation to correspond to larger museum exhibitions.

bitions for years to come. In the spring of 1946, after receiving word through the British Consulate in Washington, D.C., that officials in Great Britain had agreed to the idea of an exhibition in principle, Rich and Mr. and Mrs. Chauncey McCormick sailed for Europe to finalize the plans. Rich worked closely with the directors of several London museums, particularly with Sir Kenneth Clark of the National Gallery. With the war having so recently ended, arrangements for packing, shipping, and insuring the works to be sent required endless tact and perseverance.[49] "Masterpieces of English Painting: Hogarth, Constable, Turner" opened at the Art Institute in October 1946, and was subsequently shown at the Metropolitan Museum (see figs. 20 and 21). The exhibit was drawn exclusively from the public and private collections of Great Britain, particularly the National Gallery, the Victoria and Albert Museum, and the collection of His Majesty King George VI.

The results were well worth the trouble. The show caused the sort of excitement at the Art Institute that had not been experienced since the Century of Progress exhibition in 1933, and attendance during the show's two-month run exceeded all expectations. On an almost daily basis, the local papers ran stories about the exhibition. In conjunction with the show, Kuh mounted an explanatory exhibition in the Gallery of Art Interpretation entitled "Constable and Turner: The Road to Impressionism." To further enhance the educational value of the show, Rich organized a two-day symposium that included lectures by Sir Kenneth Clark of the National Gallery in London, Andrew Ritchie of the Albright Art Gallery in Buffalo, and W. G. Constable of the Museum of Fine Arts, Boston.

Chicagoans displayed an almost insatiable appetite for these precursors of today's blockbuster exhibitions, and Rich and his staff struggled to keep pace. In the ensuing years, they arranged shows such as "Masterpieces of French Tapestry" (1948); "From Colony to Nation: Exhibition of American Painting, Silver, and Architecture from 1650 to the War of 1812" (1949); "Twentieth-Century Art: From the Louise and Walter Arensberg Collection" (1949); "Masterpieces of Art from Vienna" (1950); and "Masterpieces of Religious Art" (1954). In addition to these "masterpiece" exhibitions, Rich, as Chief Curator of the Department of Painting and Sculpture, put together impressive retrospective exhibitions of the masters of late nineteenth- and early twentieth-century art. In cooperation with the Metropolitan Museum, he organized and wrote the catalogues for many important exhibitions, including "Vincent van Gogh: Painting and Drawings" (1950) and "Cézanne: Paintings, Watercolors, and Drawings" (1952). During this same period, Rich was bringing to Chicago retrospective exhibitions of major artists that had been organized by other institutions, particularly The Museum of Modern Art, with shows devoted to the art of Marc Chagall (1947) and Henri Matisse (1952).

While these exhibitions enjoyed both public and critical success, one—the "Fifty-Eighth Annual Exhibition of American Painting and Sculpture" of 1947—did not. The Art Institute's Annual American exhibition was a juried show inaugurated in 1888 with the intention of displaying the latest trends in contemporary American art. Because they were open to any American artist who chose to enter, the resulting juried exhibitions were often a hodgepodge of styles and uneven in their level of accomplishment. Departing from this tradition, Rich decided that the 1947 Annual Exhibition would be devoted strictly to works of abstract and Surrealist art by American artists, making the Art Institute the first American museum to stage such a show. In assembling the exhibition, the curators in charge, Kuh and Sweet, traveled by car over twenty-four thousand miles, visiting studios, universities, and galleries in order to seek out artists who were working in these styles, but who were largely unknown.[50] Artists from twenty-nine states were represented, over one-third of whom had never previously exhibited in a museum or gallery. Also, as Kuh pointed out in her catalogue essay, forty-two of the artists were women, a notable increase over past Annuals.

Despite a carefully planned public-relations campaign and strong supporting educational programs, the exhibition aroused a storm of criticism, largely incited by the Chicago press. In the catalogue, Rich and the curators had attempted to soften the public's reaction to the show by placing abstraction and Surrealism in an appropriate historical context. Rich invoked the 1913 Armory Show as evidence that Chicago had always led the way in accepting the most difficult modern art.[51] Despite these attempts to rationalize the exhibition, criticism was harsh. C. J. Bulliett of the *Chicago Daily News* wrote of the "fantastic abstractions and nightmarish surrealism," which he felt demonstrated the "poverty and feeble imitations of a score of foreign isms." Alfred Barr, who had served on the jury that awarded the exhibition prizes, however, rushed to the museum's defense, declaring that "as one of the greatest museums in the country to have been host to this sort of thing in the face of popular reluctance and a great deal of hostility on the part of the people is a wonderful thing for the Institute to do."[52]

The controversy surrounding the 1947 Annual Exhibition followed quickly on the heels of a similar national situation. In 1946, the State Department had organized an exhibition that was to tour the world to show what advancements had been made in American art during the

FIGURE 22. Left to right, Rich, Mr. and Mrs. Arnold Maremont, Kuh (seated), and Dr. Piero Guadagnini, the Italian Consul General, at the Art Institute, 1956. Mr. and Mrs. Maremont underwrote the Art Institute's participation in the 1956 Venice Biennale, for which Kuh organized the United States Pavilion.

war. The show, which included several abstract works, was well received abroad, but was vehemently protested by conservative American artists and politicians. The show was withdrawn from circulation and returned to the United States after it was denounced by President Harry Truman.

Amid the uproar and name calling, Rich emerged as a voice of reason in an article he published in the February 1948 issue of *The Atlantic Monthly.* Entitled "Freedom of the Brush," the article was arranged in three sections. The first section supplied ample evidence that abstract painting was far from a dying trend, as many critics predicted, and was gaining in popularity among young artists. The second section provided an extended historical discussion of abstraction in America, beginning with the Armory Show and continuing through to the mass immigration of European artists to the United States during World War II. In the final section, Rich took on the critics of abstract art, particularly the right-wing politicians who were using it as ammunition to denounce communism. Rich pointed out the irony of this situation, writing that "at the very moment when our abstractionists and surrealists are being attacked as Communists, the Communists themselves are accusing such artists of serving the selfish interest of the bourgeoisie and catering to their decadent and perverted tastes."[53]

The following year, Rich found himself being accused of communist leanings by Congressman George A. Dondero of Michigan (see, in this issue, the essay by Naomi Sawelson-Gorse, p. 88). In a speech delivered to the House of Representatives on August 16, 1949, Dondero quoted extensively from Rich's *Atlantic Monthly* article as evidence that Rich was an encourager of "international art thugs" who were set on destroying American art and principles. Dondero mistakenly denounced Rich as having been a Harvard student of Paul Sachs, whom he accused of turning the Fogg Museum into a place where an "effeminate tribe" was trained "in jamming this art trash down the throats of the public."[54] Rich refused to comment on these charges, and was given solid support by the Board of Trustees. Nevertheless, the continuing public resistance to modernism was dispiriting to him, and he felt that it was in part the fault of museums for not providing adequate tools for nurturing public acceptance.

Throughout the 1950s, Rich's time was devoted increasingly to administrative duties and less to dealing directly with exhibitions and the permanent collection.[55] Because he was a highly visible member of the art community, his counsel was constantly being sought by outside groups, and he served on the boards of several local and national organizations.[56] Among the multitude of projects that demanded his attention at the museum, fundraising was beginning to play a more prominent role. In the past, the museum director had very little responsibility for raising money, this being seen as the domain of the trustees. Furthermore, until the war, most of the museum's operating budget had been covered by bequests, endowments, and gifts from a small group of benefactors and trustees. Following the war, however, this changed. The increasing number of programs had raised expenses so much that, by 1951, the Art Institute was forced for the first time to appeal directly to the public for money.

The fund drive, which lasted almost two years and successfully reached its goal of nearly two million dollars, was supervised by the trustees, but Rich was closely involved. This money was desperately needed for urgent rehabilitation of the museum's antiquated physical plant and for a long-deferred refurbishment of the galleries. Photographs of the museum dating from the late 1940s and early 1950s demonstrate that the galleries were in a poor state. Also at this time, the museum began planning for a new addition to house administrative offices. After an extended legal battle, money from the B. F. Ferguson Fund was made available in 1955 to fund this project (see fig. 23).[57]

Rich's growing dissatisfaction with his job at the Art Institute became clear by the mid-1950s. In 1955, in an address before the American Federation of Arts, Rich discussed his feelings. The address, "Letter to Paul," took the form of an older museum director writing to a younger one, passing on advice and voicing his concerns regarding the role of art museums in American culture. Rich was brutally honest about the failure of museums to present art in a way that would have a direct impact on the lives of the public. While he acknowledged the "ever-increasing number of art museums. . .in America, the rise in the sale of art books and reproductions, the mass attendance at exhibitions," he despaired at the lack of "the slightest sign of improvement in the. . .design of our houses" or of the "cars pouring from our assembly lines." As Rich explained, "We have led millions to art museums to titillate, amuse and delight them, but we have failed in not making more clear the connection between the various visual arts." Despite his disillusionment with the profession, however, Rich had not abandoned hope, encouraging his audience to continue its efforts even in the face of "falling incomes, local red-hunts for Communist artists, overwork and dragons masquerading as donors."[58]

Rich's Final Years

Rich's last year at the Art Institute was one of triumph and controversy. On the one hand, he finally realized an exhibition that had been postponed for nearly ten years. On the other, Rich found himself once again the victim of a narrow-minded public, a reactionary press, and, on this occasion, a partially unsupportive Board of Trustees.

The exhibition he succeeded in putting together was on Georges Seurat, and was organized with The Museum of Modern Art (see fig. 24). Rich had been trying to mount the show since 1949, but had to defer it continually for several reasons, primarily lack of time to devote to the project. At last, in 1955, the two museums established dates for the exhibition. While the costs of the project were to be shared, the Art Institute was the principal organizer.[59] Over the following two years, Rich was heavily involved in arranging the show. He made two trips to Europe to secure loans, and he wrote countless letters cajoling reluctant owners to lend their works to the exhibition. Rich wrote the catalogue, expanding

FIGURE 23. Allan McNab, assistant director of the Art Institute, with a model of the museum's buildings, c. 1958. McNab was hired by the trustees in 1956 to help Rich cope with the increasing administrative duties imposed upon the director's office.

upon his research done nearly thirty years before for his book *Seurat and the Evolution of "La Grande Jatte."* The result of his effort was the largest exhibition until that time devoted to Seurat. Rich had been able to secure Frederic Bartlett's permission to lend the *Grande Jatte* to the New York museum for the occasion, the only time since its accession that this painting had left the museum. With only a few exceptions, the show brought together all of Seurat's major paintings and over one hundred drawings. The exhibition, the last one Rich organized as director of the Art Institute, opened in Chicago in January 1958 and was enormously successful.

In New York, the exhibition opened on March 24, 1958, to an equally enthusiastic reception. Its success was marred, however, by a fire that broke out in the galleries of The Museum of Modern Art on April 15. Although the *Grande Jatte* was rescued unscathed, this near catastrophe caused the Art Institute trustees to decide against ever lending this work again.

The controversy of Rich's last year resulted from his refusal to display at the museum an exhibition of paintings by Sir Winston Churchill. The show of thirty-five paintings had been organized and circulated by an American greeting-card company and was seen by vast numbers of people at the Metropolitan Museum and the Smithsonian Institution, Washington, D.C., among other venues. When the exhibition was offered to the Art Institute, many of the trustees were enthusiastic about it—apparently because of the publicity it would generate rather than for its artistic merits. Nevertheless, Rich's decision not to show it prevailed, with strong support from his staff. His reasoning, as reported in the press, was that, despite Churchill's political greatness and popularity, he was an amateur artist and the museum did not display the works of amateurs.[60] Public rage over the decision was fanned by the press, which wrote scathingly of Rich's "hoity-toity" attitude.[61] This episode also revived the public chastisement of Rich and the Art Institute for showing abstract art rather than the bland landscapes that were Churchill's specialty.

The situation worsened on April 28, 1958, when Rich announced that he was resigning his position at the Art Institute to become director of the Worcester Art Museum in Massachusetts. The Churchill controversy and Rich's resignation became linked in people's minds, since many felt that he was leaving in response to the situation. Rich strongly denied this, and indeed the record proves that the Worcester job was offered and accepted by March 31, 1958, weeks before the Churchill debacle. Rich cited as his reasons for resigning his disinclination to perform increasing administrative duties at the Art Institute and the fact that the Worcester job would allow him more freedom for research, writing, and travel. The very Chicago newspapers that only a few days earlier had been severely criticizing Rich now mourned his departure as a "staggering blow" to Chicago culture.[62]

Speculation has continued on the matter of Rich's resignation. While he was clearly anxious to free himself of endless administrative chores, it seems that some agreeable arrangement could have been worked out with the trustees. There is evidence that many of the trustees were not disappointed by Rich's resignation. Since the late 1940s, younger trustees, who were also active collectors of twentieth-century art, wanted a stronger voice for themselves in shaping the direction of the museum, particularly in the area of acquisitions.[63]

While Rich's departure was surprising, it was not the only one that the Art Institute had to endure at this time. In a period of about two years, the museum lost much of the staff that Rich had so diligently assembled over the previous two decades. Carl Schniewind, who had achieved so much in the Department of Prints and Drawings, died in Italy in 1957, while on a research and

FIGURE 24. Rich with his wife, Bertha, at the opening of the Art Institute's Georges Seurat exhibition, January 1958. This exhibition, co-organized with The Museum of Modern Art, was the culmination of Rich's many years of research into Seurat's work.

FIGURE 25. Katharine Kuh, Marc Chagall, and Rich standing in front of Chagall's painting *Birth* (1911/12), at the Art Institute, 1958.

buying trip. Meyric Rogers left in July 1958 to take a position as Curator of the Garvan Collection of American Decorative Arts at the Yale University Art Gallery. George Culler, who had headed Museum Education since 1955, left in June 1958 to become director of the San Francisco Museum of Art. Finally, Katharine Kuh, whose name had been mentioned by the press as a possible successor to Rich, left in 1959, moving to New York, where she became the art correspondent for the *Saturday Review,* as well as a highly successful independent curator and writer. She was succeeded by A. James Speyer. John Maxon, director of the Rhode Island School of Design, came to Chicago in late 1959 to replace Rich.

As for Rich, he went on to have a very distinguished career at the Worcester Art Museum, where he remained as director until 1970. In 1960–61, he was a visiting lecturer at Harvard University. Many of his achievements at Worcester paralleled his earlier achievements in Chicago: he doubled the size of the Education Department staff, extensively increased the holdings of the Department of Twentieth-Century Art, developed a photography collection, and more than doubled the museum's membership.

Upon leaving Worcester, Rich retired to New York City, where, among his other activities, he served as a trustee of the Solomon R. Guggenheim Museum. His wife, Bertha, had died in Worcester in 1968. Rich died of pancreatic cancer in New York City on October 17, 1976. A short time after his death, a memorial service was held in the rotunda of the Guggenheim Museum. Among testimonials from Rich's many friends and colleagues, the artist Margo Hoff read a eulogy written by Georgia O'Keeffe, who was unable to attend.

Today Daniel Catton Rich's name is hardly known. Even within the Art Institute itself, people are unfamiliar with his achievements, despite the fact that so many of the museum's current programs owe a large debt to his foresight and energy. His taste and that of his staff have had a lasting influence on nearly every aspect of the Art Institute. Curatorial departments that were established under his directorship, such as Africa, Oceania, and the Americas, have continued to flourish, largely because of the strong foundations he helped lay. Likewise, the Department of Conservation resulted from Rich's initiatives, as did many other departments that support the basic mission of the museum. Innovations like these, coupled with the many important works of art that he acquired for the museum, serve to make Rich's directorship one of the most ambitious and important in the Art Institute's history. As the museum passed from an older, more conservative way of approaching its collections and programs, it was fortunate to have a leader of Daniel Catton Rich's intelligence and vision.

The Art Institute of Chicago and the Arensberg Collection

NAOMI SAWELSON-GORSE
University of California, Santa Barbara

From October 20 to December 18, 1949, the special-exhibition galleries on the second floor of The Art Institute of Chicago's east wing were filled with nearly two hundred works by fifty-one, primarily European, modern artists.[1] "Twentieth-Century Art: From the Louise and Walter Arensberg Collection" was, by all accounts, a landmark exhibition. It was significant not only because of the superlative quality of the art and the incredible number of works included by the Romanian sculptor Constantin Brancusi and the French avant-garde artist Marcel Duchamp, but also because it was the first time the Arensbergs' collection had been displayed in a museum.

The artists represented were truly a roll call of the major names in the earlier twentieth-century avant-garde working in the period's most important styles, from Cubism to Dada and Surrealism. The roster of names, in addition to Brancusi and Duchamp, included Braque, Dalí, Ernst, Kandinsky, Klee, Miró, and Picasso. This was not the first time that some of their works had been seen in Chicago. For example, Duchamp's *Nude Descending a Staircase, No. 2* (see fig. 16), the *cause scandale* of the famed Armory Show, which had been staged at the Art Institute in 1913, was in the exhibition, along with several other paintings and sculptures that had been included in the earlier event.[2] Also on display were works shown at the Art Institute in 1922 and again in 1932–33 that had once been part of a major Chicago collection of avant-garde art belonging to Arthur Jerome Eddy.[3]

Few Chicagoans, however, were familiar with the collectors Walter and Louise Arensberg (fig. 2). Having no ties to the city, and living far away, in Hollywood, California, the couple was rarely in the public eye.[4] The Arensbergs had two obsessions: the acquisition of art, mostly modern and pre-Columbian works; and the gathering of incontrovertible proof that Francis Bacon, Lord Chancellor of England in the early seventeenth century, wrote the plays and poems usually attributed to William Shakespeare.

The Arensbergs, although not millionaires, were financially comfortable. Louise's prudent management of her family inheritance enabled the couple to acquire art—numbering some one thousand items by the time of the Art Institute's exhibition—after Walter had squandered most of his wealth on bad debts and poor investments. Nonetheless, Walter was able to support a staff to aid him in his Baconian research and to print privately several books and pamphlets on the Shakespeare-authorship controversy.[5] His assistants, usually three, spent their days in a room in the Arensbergs' home, decodifying Shakespearean and Baconian texts, producing reams of papers filled with numerical and cryptographic calculations. In order to ensure the continuation of this research, the Arensbergs established The Francis Bacon Foundation in the mid-1930s as a non-profit institution; it continues to this day in Claremont, California.

The constant flow of visitors who made the transcontinental trek to Hollywood to meet the Arensbergs and

FIGURE 1. Foyer of the Arensbergs' Hollywood home, 1944, photographed by Fred R. Dapprich. The Constantin Brancusi ensemble combines the sculptor's 1915 wooden *Doorway* and his 1916 polished brass *Princess X,* both today in the Louise and Walter Arensberg Collection at the Philadelphia Museum of Art, with a selection of pre-Columbian pieces. Photo courtesy of Philadelphia Museum of Art, Arensberg Archives.

FIGURE 2. Louise Stevens Arensberg (1879–1953) and Walter Conrad Arensberg (1878–1954) with the French avant-garde artist Marcel Duchamp (1887–1968), during his first visit to the couple's Hollywood home, August 17, 1936, photographed by Beatrice Wood. Photo courtesy of Arensberg Archives, Francis Bacon Library.

see their collection was immediately accosted by a visual cacophony (figs. 1 and 3–7). The dimly lit, crowded rooms of their two-story house were crammed with modern works and pre-Columbian artifacts. Hung closely together, rising from floor to ceiling, the works occupied hallways and staircases and were positioned precariously on any available surface, whether doors, doorways, or bathroom walls. Oriental rugs were piled high, sometimes four to five, cushioning one's footsteps. For The Art Institute of Chicago's director Daniel Catton Rich and curator Katharine Kuh, who were among the guests in the late 1940s, the atmosphere the Arensbergs had created was "magical."[6]

Quiet, seemingly aloof, but actually shy, Louise was thin and frail, with wisps of white hair haloing her face. Then riddled with cancer, she constantly wrung her hands, trying to alleviate the pain that consumed her. Walter, in contrast, was charming, energetic, and buoyant, belying his age (both he and his wife were in their seventies) and his many illnesses with a sharp intelligence and scholarly erudition. He was as outspoken and mercurial as his wife was socially withdrawn. The childless couple seemed a most unlikely duo to have committed their energies and funds to what some called complete nonsense, if not outright insanity.[7]

Mary Louise Stevens, who was usually addressed by her middle name, although her close friends called her "Lou," was born in Dresden in 1879. She and her two brothers grew up amidst the wealth of their maternal family, founders of the later well-known J. P. Stevens firm in the textile centers of North Andover and Ludlow, Massachusetts. Louise attended school in Dresden, where she excelled as a concert pianist and as a soprano. Not long after Louise returned to Ludlow upon completing her studies, her family life was disrupted by the deaths of her parents. Several years later, in 1907, she married Walter Conrad Arensberg. They moved to Boston, where Walter had already established himself as a writer with the *Boston Transcript.*

Walter's father, a liquor merchant who later became part owner of a crucible steel factory in Pittsburgh, Pennsylvania, was descended from Germans who had immigrated to the United States in the mid-nineteenth century and had quickly become successful in industry and other occupations. Walter grew up in Oakmont, an affluent suburb of Pittsburgh. He and his brothers attended Harvard; Walter and his brother Charles were elected class poets of their respective years (1900 and 1901). After a *Wanderjahr* in Europe and a short stint teaching English at Harvard, Walter worked for the *New York Evening Post,* eventually leaving New York for Boston. In between the hectic duties of a stringer reporter, he managed to continue writing poetry, some of which was published in two books, *Poems* (1914) and *Idols* (1916).

Walter was assigned to review the International Exhibition of Modern Art during its run at New York's 69th Regiment Armory in February 1913, before it traveled to Chicago's Art Institute and Boston's Copley Hall (see, in this issue, the essay by Andrew Martinez). This exhibition not only changed the course of art in the United States, but also the Arensbergs' lives. None of their previous knowledge about art prepared them for the shock of the Armory Show, which "hit" Walter "between wind and water," a friend recalled.[8] In later years, Walter circulated the probably exaggerated story that he "actually forgot to go home for several days."[9] Louise saw the Armory Show with her husband and was equally confounded. She wrote to a friend that the sculpture by the German artist Wilhelm Lehmbruck was "almost the mildest atrocity in the exhibition," and that

FIGURE 3. View of living room, toward sun room, in the Arensbergs' Hollywood home, c. 1944, photographed by Fred R. Dapprich. James Thrall Soby, who curated many exhibitions at New York's Museum of Modern Art, thought the display of objects in the Arensbergs' home was uniquely successful: "In these days . . . when . . . we tend to isolate and canonize the work of art, it is sobering to think upon a successful exception to the rule. The Arensberg pictures stand belligerently close together, but they do not fight. Their hanging breaks every museum precept of height, space and light, but you see them clearly, one by one, and remember them in detail for a long time afterward" (Soby, "Marcel Duchamp in the Arensberg Collection," *View* 5, 1 [1945], p. 11). Photo courtesy of Philadelphia Museum of Art, Arensberg Archives.

FIGURE 6. Main staircase in the Arensbergs' Hollywood home, 1944/49, photographed by Fred R. Dapprich. Photo courtesy of Philadelphia Museum of Art, Arensberg Archives.

FIGURE 7. Second-floor guest bedroom in the Arensbergs' Hollywood home, 1944/49, photographed by Fred R. Dapprich. Photo courtesy of Philadelphia Museum of Art, Arensberg Archives.

FIGURE 4. View of sun room, toward living room, in the Arensbergs' Hollywood home, c. 1944, photographed by Fred R. Dapprich. Photo courtesy of Philadelphia Museum of Art, Arensberg Archives.

FIGURE 5. Dining-room fireplace in the Arensbergs' Hollywood home, 1944/49, photographed by Fred R. Dapprich. Photo courtesy of Philadelphia Museum of Art, Arensberg Archives.

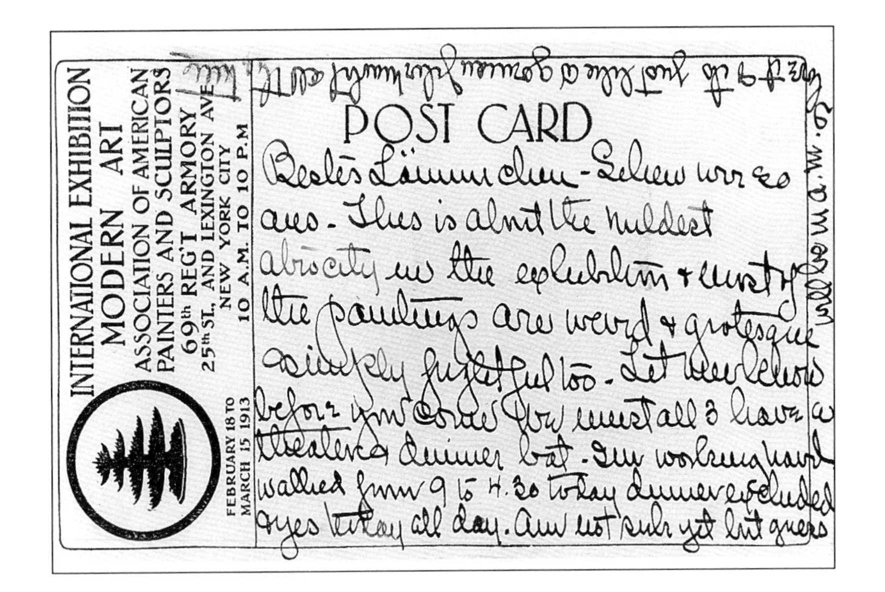

INTERNATIONAL EXHIBITION
MODERN ART
ASSOCIATION OF AMERICAN
PAINTERS AND SCULPTORS
69th REG'T ARMORY
25th ST. AND LEXINGTON AVE.
NEW YORK CITY
10 A.M. TO 10 P.M.
FEBRUARY 18 TO
MARCH 15 1913

POST CARD

FIGURE 8. On a postcard, addressed to an unidentified friend, showing Wilhelm Lehmbruck's *Kneeling Woman*, Louise Arensberg disparagingly described the modern art at the 1913 Armory Show. While she called this sculpture "the mildest atrocity in the exhibition," she quickly changed her point of view to one of complete commitment. Eventually, she and her husband acquired about a dozen of the most controversial and publicized works in the show. Photo courtesy of Arensberg Archives, Francis Bacon Library.

she was horrified by "most of the paintings," finding them "weird & grotesque & simply frightful too" (see fig. 8).[10] Their feelings reflected those of the huge crowds who saw the exhibition. Duchamp's paintings, in particular, and the other European modernist examples, in general, visually assaulted the public. Seemingly without a basis in the history of art or aesthetics, these works represented to them discontinuity and unintelligibility.

But the Arensbergs' adverse reactions were short-lived. Under the guidance of one of the exhibition's organizers, the American artist and writer Walter Pach, Louise and Walter began their first foray into purchasing the very objects they previously had found baffling. Eventually, Cubist works of 1912–13 formed the majority of twentieth-century items in their collection. The Arensbergs also acquired about one dozen of the Armory Show's most controversial and publicized paintings and sculptures, including works by Brancusi, Duchamp, and Francis Picabia.

Moreover, Louise and Walter became patrons of those artists, as well. Picabia and Albert Gleizes, for instance, were just two of the many French émigré artists who participated in the almost daily gatherings and nightly soirées held at the Arensbergs' New York apartment at 33 West 67th Street, their residence after they moved from the Boston area in 1914. The most important member of the Arensbergs' New York salon, and its catalyst, was Marcel Duchamp, who began a lifelong friendship with Walter Arensberg in the summer of 1915, during the first of his many visits to the United States.[11] Like Walter, Duchamp played chess and word games, cerebral pursuits similar to his art. The two men quickly formed a bond into which Louise, while supportive of the artist, could never truly enter. Duchamp replaced Pach as the Arensbergs' adviser and mentor.

Already by this time, Duchamp had removed himself entirely from the art market by handling the sale (and therefore controlling the monetary value) of his own works. He never had an art dealer in the contemporary sense, where an artist enters into a contractual agreement with someone who then becomes the sole agent of the artist's productions. Rather, Duchamp either sold or gave his works to a small circle of friends, family members, and other intimate associates, earmarking specific works for certain individuals. This total control, Duchamp explained, was a result of his small output, and his art, therefore, "had no right to be speculated upon, that is, to travel from one collection to another and get dispersed."[12]

Duchamp nonetheless had no compunction about dealing in the works of other artists, whether or not they were his contemporaries. The Arensbergs, for instance, were the beneficiaries of Duchamp's active dealing in other artists' productions; moreover, the quantity of modern art the Arensbergs bought from Duchamp exceeded that which the couple purchased from established art dealers.[13] The couple would also send the artist money for expenses not directly related to these art purchases. In effect, therefore, Duchamp became an employee of the Arensbergs. And the Arensbergs, in turn, became Duchamp's foremost American champions and collectors.

Walter referred to himself as Duchamp's "silent guard," quietly gathering the artist's works, and reveling in their mystery.[14] This private experience was finally extended to a wide audience by the Art Institute's 1949 exhibition. The public could see the full range of Duchamp's oeuvre, from his Cubist-inspired paintings that stress motion to his appropriation of every-day objects into "readymades," and his frequent replications of his own works. The museum director Henry Hopkins, then a student at the School of the Art Institute, recalled that seeing Duchamp's works for the first time at the exhibition "gave me, at the beginning of my career, the opportunity to be free, to get away from what I thought art was and to contemplate what art could be."[15]

But it was not only Duchamp's works that provided a revelation. Until the Art Institute's exhibition, the completeness of the Arensbergs' vision for their collection was never fully comprehended and appreciated. The Arensbergs' selectivity, the overall quality of their collection, and the concentration on modern art—particularly Cubism—was repeatedly commented upon by reviewers. Certainly, the presentation at the Art Institute of the Arensbergs' collection aided in these assessments. For Duchamp and others who had visited the Arensbergs' Hollywood home, where individual art objects vied for space, the installation by the Art Institute's Associate Curator of Painting and Sculpture, Katharine Kuh, gave the works "a new life" (see fig. 9).[16]

Separating paintings from sculptures, Kuh created spaces for major movements, such as Surrealism, devoting larger wall areas to works by individual artists, such as Picasso. Two galleries were dedicated to the two men whose works the Arensbergs especially revered: Brancusi and Duchamp. The exhibition ended with photographs of artists represented in the collection, such as Edward Steichen's portrait of Duchamp.[17]

Duchamp, who had installed many exhibitions himself, was impressed by Kuh's spacious arrangement of Brancusi's sculpture and his work. The artist was equally admiring of the indirect lighting that Kuh had used:

> All the rooms are lighted from an entirely luminous ceiling (ground glass) which give evenly distributed daylight or electric light. That even distribution of the light is very becoming to the paintings and sculpture (as compared with the ordinary spotlighting). In fact you are not conscious of the source of light.[18]

With ample spacing and indirect lighting, the installation not only gave a new vitality to individual works but also the collection as a whole and as compared to the Art Institute's modern holdings. "In these new surroundings," Duchamp observed, the Arensbergs' collection "stands out like a block apart from the already classic Impressionists" whose works were hung in the museum's permanent galleries.[19]

Throngs of visitors saw the exhibition. Because the Arensberg collection was shown only at the Art Institute,

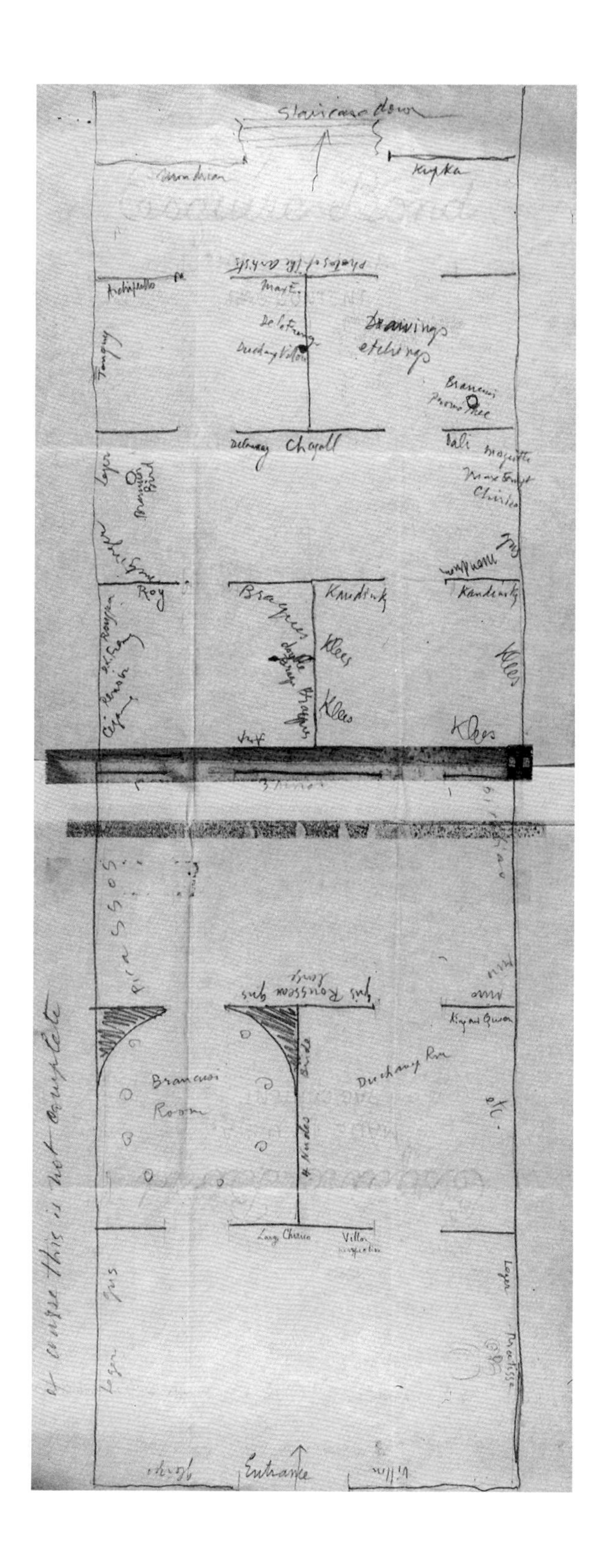

FIGURE 9. Marcel Duchamp's drawing of the installation of "Twentieth-Century Art: From the Louise and Walter Arensberg Collection" at the Art Institute, held in galleries 52–61 from October 20–December 18, 1949. Photo courtesy of Arensberg Archives, Francis Bacon Library.

"attendance," a local reporter noted, was "remarkable. Numerous conducted tours by colleges and universities within the city as well as from surrounding territory [contributed] to the thousands of individual visits."[20] Eager listeners packed the Art Institute's Fullerton Hall for four Friday evening lectures given by different speakers on various aspects of the collection, and gallery talks were presented throughout the run of the show.[21]

Some who had found modern art distasteful were suddenly mesmerized, overwhelmed, and forced to revise long-held views. Francis Henry Taylor, director of New York's Metropolitan Museum of Art, who often publicly disparaged contemporary and modern art, was "moved. . .deeply" by the exhibition; he spent an entire day looking at the works of art and found them, much to his surprise, "uniformly high [in] quality."[22] Even for the *Chicago Tribune*'s art critic, Eleanor Jewett, a perennial foe of all things modern, the shock of the by-now *old* avant-garde had lessened, leaving her to wonder how and why Duchamp's infamous *Nude Descending a Staircase* "could ever have shattered anyone's calm" when seen in the 1913 Armory Show.[23]

FIGURE 10. Paul Rand (American, born 1914), cover for the exhibition catalogue *Twentieth-Century Art: From the Louise and Walter Arensberg Collection.*

The accompanying exhibition catalogue (fig. 10), designed by the innovative graphic artist Paul Rand, was equally applauded.[24] Profusely illustrated, reproducing many works never before published, the volume was the first printed record of the collection and remains, even today, the most comprehensive listing. An essay by Rich and Kuh summarized the Arensbergs' collection in all of its diversity. Rich and Kuh also contributed articles on Brancusi and Duchamp, respectively.

By all accounts, the exhibition was a great success. Its enthusiastic critical and public reception somewhat offset the political attacks that had recently beset both Rich and Duchamp. They each had been denounced as communists or fellow travelers by the antiradical crusader George A. Dondero, a Republican congressman from Michigan. In an August 16, 1949, speech on the floor of the United States House of Representatives, "Modern Art Shackled to Communism," Dondero equated all modern art with communist propaganda, and unjustly accused Duchamp of being one of the "four leaders of the Cubist group," who were all "reds," and Rich of being a "fellow traveler." Duchamp, as well as other émigré artists who were welcomed into the United States in recent years, were now in the country, Dondero proclaimed, "to aid in the destruction of our standards and traditions" and Rich and his like were active participants in this process.[25]

While the Art Institute and Duchamp weathered the anticommunist storm, the jubilation about the Arensberg show, as Kuh later recalled, belied one of the "saddest, saddest" episodes in her professional life.[26] A major proponent of modernism, Kuh, along with Rich, had long been aware of the seminal importance and uniqueness of the Arensbergs' collection and anxious not only to exhibit it at the Art Institute but to secure it for the museum as well.[27] After years devoted to forming friendships with both Arensbergs, cataloguing the collection, staging its exhibition in Chicago, and negotiating with the collectors for their holdings to come permanently to the Art Institute, Kuh saw her hopes dashed and the friendships ended.

Four years before, in April 1945, the possibility of this major bequest coming to the Art Institute looked promising. When Rich visited the Arensbergs in Hollywood, they had a tentative discussion about the Art Institute mounting a show of the entire collection. Besides the European and American modern works, the Arensbergs also had contemporary Mexican art and pre-Columbian, Mesoamerican, African, and Native American objects, as well as early Americana, ranging in size, uniqueness, and rarity from paintings by Paul Cézanne to an Egyptian mummy cloth and countless small spearheads.

Certainly, such an exhibition would be a mammoth undertaking, but it would also surely be a coup for the Art Institute to be the first museum to show the collection and would give Chicago an edge over all the other competitors for the collection. Over the years, the Arensbergs discussed the disposition of their collection with over thirty institutions, ranging from university art galleries (such as Harvard University's Fogg Art Museum) to major museums (like New York's Metropolitan Museum of Art), as well as colleges that wanted to establish vital art programs (for example, the University of Minnesota).[28]

Rich accepted the terms that the Arensbergs insisted upon, according to which the museum was granted "permission to exhibit the entire collection, with the condition that the Institute would provide a catalogue for the entire collection." The show would enable the Arensbergs "to see how the whole collection, as a composite of so many sharply contrasting elements, would appear in a museum installation,"[29] and the catalogue would provide them with a much-needed record of information on the objects.

A public viewing of the collection—at the Art Institute, if not also at other museums, such as the San Diego Museum of Art and New York's Museum of Modern Art, which were also vying for the opportunity to show these works—was in accord with the Arensbergs' commitment to promoting the modernist aesthetic. Although they had opted to physically isolate themselves from major art centers when they moved permanently to Hollywood from New York, the couple had always made their collection accessible in California by allowing visitors in their home and by agreeing to numerous loans to local, as well as national, exhibitions. Now they were trying to make "their children" (as they often referred to their collection) even more visible.

Not until 1948 were more definite plans formalized for the Art Institute's show. Much of the delay was caused by the University of California. The Arensbergs had bequeathed their collection to the university in the fall of 1944 with the proviso that a suitable museum to house it be erected on the Los Angeles campus after World War II. The museum, however, was not built. The regents of the university never asked for funding from the state, undermining, through their lack of action, the realization of the museum within the agreed-upon time limit. The bequest of the Arensbergs' collection to the university was nullified officially in the summer of 1947.[30] Shortly thereafter, the Arensbergs became involved in another project: the Modern Institute of Art in Beverly Hills, which they cosponsored along with other local collectors of modern and contemporary art. The Arensbergs saw what was to be the first modern art museum in the Los Angeles area as the probable home for their art. They stopped considering such a bequest, however, when the new museum's financial instability and quarrels among its sponsors made it clear that the institution could not be sustained. Nonetheless, the couple postponed the Art Institute's exhibition date from the fall of 1948 to the fall of 1949 in order to accommodate promised loans to the fledgling Los Angeles museum.

The Arensbergs asked the Art Institute's director to suggest an appropriate permanent repository for their collection. Rich, naturally, recommended his own institution. The Arensbergs' collection, which he considered "the most intelligent and beautifully chosen [one] of twentieth century art in the world," would not only "be best enjoyed and used" at the Art Institute, Rich emphasized in his letters to the couple, but would also supply the museum with "many of the links and landmarks which [they] have collected" and that the museum lacked.[31]

Despite all that the Art Institute was offering the couple—an exhibition and catalogue of their entire collection—tensions occurred almost from the very outset of preparations for the show. In late June 1948, for instance, when Kuh arrived at the Arensbergs' to begin cataloguing the collection "Mrs. A[rensberg] was shocked to see" her because the couple had "evidently . . .decided that the deal was off."[32] One day, Kuh would be received with open arms, and the next she would be shunned.

Kuh was constantly bewildered by the quixotic behavior of her hosts and by endless misunderstandings. The Arensbergs' insistence, for example, that, while she catalogued the collection the works remain in place —whether they were in the stairwells or hanging in the bathrooms—forced Kuh to scamper over ladders, couches, and chairs in order to obtain necessary measurements. Thus, the dimensions published in the catalogue are, in part, estimates that Kuh was often forced to make. The Arensbergs' unpredictability continued throughout the subsequent year-and-a-half history of the exhibition. As Kuh put it, "'the picture changes' every hour on the hour."[33]

Yet, during her last sojourn with the Arensbergs, in April 1949, Kuh was privileged to interact with the couple and their collection on a daily basis, an opportunity that no other museum person had ever had before in an official capacity. They treated her "as indulgently as a daughter."[34] Kuh was especially fascinated by Walter. She had long discussions with him about art and aesthetics and accompanied him on rounds to Los Angeles art galleries. These experiences have remained for Kuh uniquely rich and rewarding memories. She also shared the Arensbergs' excitement about recent acquisitions. Much to her amazement, two Brancusi sculptures,

ROULETTE DE MONTE CARLO
EMPRUNT DE QUINZE MILLE FRANCS 20 o/o
DIVISÉ EN 30 OBLIGATIONS DE 500 Francs CHACUNE
Remboursables au pair en trois ans par tirages artificiels
à partir du 1er Mars 1925
(Loi du 29 Juillet 1881)
OBLIGATION DE CINQ CENTS FRANCS
AU PORTEUR 20%
No 12
PARIS, LE 1er NOVEMBRE 1924
Le Président du Conseil d'Administration
Un Administrateur
ROULETTE DE MONTE-CARLO OBLIGATION No 12
Coupon d'intérêt de 25 frs
moustiquesdomestiquesdemistock

Torso of a Young Man and *The Fish,* and a large pre-Columbian stone object were purchased on a single day by the collectors from Earl Stendahl, who ran an art gallery in his large home next door to the Arensbergs.

While the physical distance between Chicago and Hollywood probably contributed to ever-increasing miscommunication, another, even more important factor was causing problems. Unknown to the Art Institute's director and his staff, the Arensbergs were negotiating for the bequeathal of their collection to the Philadelphia Museum of Art with its director, Fiske Kimball, while preparations for the Art Institute's exhibit were still ongoing. Despite almost daily letters and telephone calls between Kuh and the Arensbergs regarding details in the catalogue, the couple gave no hint that these discussions with the Philadelphia institution were occurring simultaneously.

Another point of contention was the pre-Columbian portion of the collection. While Rich had originally agreed to show forty-three pre-Columbian pieces, he and Kuh realized that this was simply too much material for one exhibition. Rich suggested that the original selection be further reduced by omitting the larger pre-Columbian works. The Arensbergs were extremely offended by Rich's proposal. Omitting the large pre-Columbian pieces would "have the effect," Walter stated, "of making the group no longer representative."[35] For that reason, the collectors decided to eliminate the pre-Columbian works entirely from the exhibition and accompanying catalogue, informing Rich and Kuh that the show would comprise only their modern holdings.[36] This decision came as a welcome relief to Rich and Kuh. Lacking in-depth expertise in the pre-Columbian area, they would have had to employ someone from outside the Art Institute to write that portion of the catalogue. Overall, Kuh felt the pre-Columbian works would detract from the impact of the show and was especially concerned about the authenticity of some of the objects. Nonetheless, with this revised agreement, neither the exhibition nor the catalogue were to include the Arensbergs' entire collection, as the couple had originally intended. Probably, had it been up to Walter, he would have canceled the show. But, apparently, the Art Institute had a defender in Louise Arensberg.

Louise opened up to Kuh when the curator visited Los Angeles in late June 1948. Almost immediately after Kuh's departure, Louise started writing her friendly, gossipy letters. She also began taking an active role in the more formal dialogue between her husband and the Art Institute, adding comments to letters Walter dictated during his long recuperation from the cerebral hemorrhage he suffered in August 1948. With Kuh's increasing involvement in the catalogue and exhibition, the Arensbergs communicated primarily with her. They clearly had confidence in her: "We are looking forward with great interest," Louise wrote to Kuh when she, her husband, and Duchamp first saw the blueprints of the galleries in which their collection would be installed, "[to] seeing how [our] pictures will look in conventional galleries intelligently hung. We are glad you are going to do it, and no one else."[37] In token of their friendship, the Arensbergs gave Kuh a *Green Box* by Duchamp, the first of three objects by the artist she would eventually own (see fig. 11).[38]

Kuh also contacted numerous artists represented in the Arensbergs' collection to ensure that information for the catalogue was accurate, such as titles and dates of works.[39] Duchamp, in particular, provided her with bountiful information and perceptive insights, since many of the Arensbergs' objects had been acquired through him. Kuh first met the artist in New York in late September 1948. It was an encounter she looked forward to "with intense interest," and it proved one of the most memorable episodes of her labors on the exhibition, resulting in her life-long connection with the artist as curator, critic, and scholar.[40] Kuh found Duchamp "kind, cordial, and most cooperative. . .as extraordinary a person as I had anticipated. Curiously," she noted, Duchamp "looks like his work, so totally resolved."[41]

Kuh was again impressed with Duchamp when her third trip to the Arensbergs coincided with his visit in mid-April 1949 (fig. 12). She was seated in the Arensbergs' living room, Kuh recalled, when he arrived:

> There and in an adjoining garden room [Duchamp] dispassionately examined everything in sight, including paintings by his colleagues and key ones he himself had produced in another life some thirty-five years earlier. . . .He looked quietly, intently —the Arensbergs nervously following his slightest move. Finally, turning to *The King and Queen,* he said, "This one still holds up." And that was all. What he thought about his other paintings he kept to himself.[42]

Significantly, the Arensbergs chose not to go to the exhibition's opening, on October 19, 1949, which Duchamp attended (see fig. 13). The Art Institute acknowledged

FIGURE 11. Marcel Duchamp (French, 1887–1968), *Obligations pour la Roulette de Monte Carlo (Monte Carlo Bond),* 1924. Photocollage on colored lithograph; 31.7 x 22.5 cm. Inscribed lower left in ink: *Rrose Sélavy.* Inscribed lower right in ink: *Marcel Duchamp.* The David and Alfred Smart Museum of Art, The University of Chicago, Gift of Katharine Kuh (1971.43). After Daniel Catton Rich, director of the Art Institute (1938–58), gave *Monte Carlo Bond* to Kuh, Duchamp wrote a dedicatory inscription to her (lower right): *Bonne chance / Chère Katharine Kuh / Marcel Duchamp / 1953.*

FIGURE 12. Duchamp standing in front of his 1912 painting *King and Queen Surrounded by Swift Nudes,* hanging above the living-room fireplace in the Arensbergs' Hollywood home, April 1949, a painting he found that, after thirty-seven years, he still admired. Photo: *Los Angeles Daily News* Morgue, Collection 1386, Department of Special Collections, University Research Library, University of California, Los Angeles.

the artist's assistance by paying for his expenses. Although Duchamp declined an invitation to speak at this time about the Arensbergs' collection and about his own work to the Society for Contemporary American Art, an organization affiliated with the Art Institute, he did agree to a press interview, held in the room devoted to his works (see fig. 14 and Appendix, pp. 96–101). While in Chicago, the artist conferred about the possibilities of the gift of the Arensbergs' collection to the Art Institute with Rich, the museum's president Chauncey McCormick, and trustee Samuel A. Marx, an architect and modern art collector.

Marx, inspired by a preview look at the exhibition, proposed first to the Arensbergs, and then to Rich, that the Art Institute's Blackstone Hall, a two-story gallery on the main floor filled with plaster casts of antique sculptures, would be ideally suited to house the collection after substantial and costly remodeling. A hastily formed committee that included Rich, Marx, and McCormick discussed the architect's proposal, the criteria for the permanent display of the Arensbergs' collection at the Art Institute, and the presentation of these points to Duchamp. While the space of Blackstone Hall was ample, the necessary funds for the proposed remodeling were not available and had to be raised. These meetings, as well as letters and telephone calls between Rich, Duchamp, Marx, and the Arensbergs, were all unofficial. The museum's board had not yet discussed the proposal.[43] Kuh, who had no knowledge of Marx's proposal or Duchamp's emissary status, later doubted that the trustees would have ever seriously considered the bequest because most were neither "enthusiastic" about modern art nor "interested in obtaining the Arensbergs' collection."[44]

Meanwhile, the ongoing discussions with the Philadelphia Museum of Art were proceeding more smoothly than those with the Art Institute. Walter was perhaps drawn to the Philadelphia Museum because of its connection to his home state of Pennsylvania. Although Arensberg and Rich had found mutual areas of interest ranging from poetry to ghosts, Fiske Kimball was able to compete by traveling often from Philadelphia to Hollywood to confer with the Arensbergs on various aspects of installing their collection at his museum, even drafting plans for its permanent display. Duchamp was involved in this dialogue as well, not only frequently corresponding with the Arensbergs on various criteria, but also commuting from New York to Philadelphia to go through the

FIGURE 13. Duchamp and Katharine Kuh during the opening of the Arensberg show on the museum's Grand Staircase, Oct. 19(?), 1949. Duchamp positioned himself and Kuh to mimic (and mirror) the figure in his *Nude Descending a Staircase, No. 2* (see fig. 16). Photo courtesy of Katharine Kuh Papers, Archives of American Art, Smithsonian Institution.

FIGURE 14. Duchamp interviewed by the press in the Duchamp room of the Arensberg exhibition at the Art Institute, Oct. 19, 1949. Note the wire recorder on the table in front of the artist. Clockwise from center: Katharine Kuh, Duchamp, Peter Pollack (the Art Institute's Public Relations Counsel), Clarence J. Bulliet (*Chicago Daily News*), Lou Spence (*Time*), Ed Barry (*Chicago Tribune*), and Cloyd Head (WMAQ). In the room (from left to right) are Duchamp's *Sketch for "Precision Optics," Boxing Match, Cemetery of Uniforms and Liveries [No. 1], Yvonne and Magdeleine Torn in Tatters,* and *Sonata.* All works in Philadelphia Museum of Art, Louise and Walter Arensberg Collection.

area proposed for the collection at the museum with Kimball and other Philadelphia Museum personnel.

The reason the Arensbergs gave for not attending the opening of the first museum showing of their collection was Walter's recent illness and his doctor's orders not to travel. But, according to Walter's research assistant Elizabeth Wrigley, they did not want to go because they had decided against presenting the collection to the Art Institute.

Duchamp pleaded with the Arensbergs to travel to Chicago for the opening, or, if not that, at least to see the much-applauded installation at a later time. Finally, the Arensbergs did consent to make the long train ride from Hollywood to Chicago, arriving on the evening of December 9, less than two weeks before the exhibition was to close. Even though they insisted that no one from the Art Institute greet them at the train, take them to the museum, or show them through the exhibition, they evidently expected nonetheless that all of these events would occur and were upset that they did not. Respecting the Arensbergs' wishes, as the Art Institute staff understood them from the couple's written and telephone communications, no one from the Art Institute's staff carried out any of these duties; the unofficial greeter was Samuel Marx, who performed all of these tasks himself.[45]

However considerate Marx's actions appeared, they were self-serving and ultimately did not help the Art Institute's cause. The architect had been the main instigator for the remodeling of Blackstone Hall and had proposed that he be commissioned to carry out the renovation; in fact, he already had drawn plans. Now he sought to gain favor with the Arensbergs, whom he hoped would designate him as the designer of the permanent installation in Blackstone Hall of their collection.

Until the Arensbergs arrived at the Art Institute, there was only praise for Kuh's installation, and only promises for the bequeathal of the couple's collection to the museum. Louise had written to Kuh that "every report" she and her husband received

> on the Chicago exhibition of our pictures emphasizes the *very* fine installation and I assure you we appreciate the time and intelligence and labor that must have gone into it. . .[Duchamp] wrote us at great length—apparently very happy about everything. We too are happy about the present and about the possible future. We hope and we really believe that things will work out to the satisfaction of everybody.[46]

But now, the Arensbergs, visiting the Art Institute with Marx, verbally expressed their displeasure with the installation. In their opinion, the temporary-exhibition area lacked the overall aesthetic quality they had envisioned. Walter was "enraged by the isolation of the sculptures from the paintings."[47] The Brancusi area, in particular, the Arensbergs found "particularly distasteful. . .on account of the flimsey [*sic*] and inappropriate ply-wood decor, and the color of the walls."[48]

When Duchamp visited Chicago briefly in order to confer with the Arensbergs, the collectors informed him, and subsequently Marx, on December 19, 1949, that the Art Institute was no longer in contention for their collection. A year later, on December 22, 1950, the Arensbergs and Duchamp, acting as board members of the Francis Bacon Foundation, the legal holder of the Arensbergs' collection, unanimously accepted the bequeathal terms presented by the Philadelphia Museum of Art.

While Rich and Kuh were devastated, their great efforts were not fruitless, either for the Arensbergs or for the Art Institute. In addition to the exhibition, catalogue, and publicity their collection received, the couple was given something equally important: an unexpected viewpoint. They reassessed dramatically their vision about the display of their collection, not only in their home but also within a museum context. This was why Duchamp had insisted that the couple visit the exhibition. "To the contrary of our showing" the pre-Columbian and African material "in the house together" with the modern paintings and sculptures, Walter wrote to Duchamp several months after the Art Institute show closed,

> it [now] should be shown in the museum in a separate gallery. Having it shown with the pictures as it is at the present time in the house was a very exciting experience for us for many years, because it created so many interesting juxtapositions. And of course we really had no alternative either, since we had no separate space. But we came to feel, at the time of the Chicago exhibition, when the paintings were all out of the house, that the sculpture that remained in solitary possession became much more impressive, and actually filled in all the space that the paintings had left empty. In a sense, we were actually . . .seeing the sculpture for the first time.[49]

Clearly, in designing its installation for the collection, the Philadelphia Museum was able to benefit from this change of heart. Regrettably, Kuh never knew the positive effect her installation had on the Arensbergs, for her relationship with them was irrevocably severed.[50] Louise Arensberg died in 1953, her husband a few months later. Nonetheless, the Art Institute was the recipient of one great artwork thanks to Duchamp. Probably attempting to ameliorate any lingering discontent on the part of the Art Institute, he, as one of the executors of Katherine Dreier's estate after her death in 1952, arranged the presentation to the museum of a single item from Dreier's personal collection, Brancusi's *Leda* (fig. 15).[51]

Not one local newspaper reported what happened behind the scenes during the exhibition. Only Aline

FIGURE 15. Constantin Brancusi (Romanian, 1876–1957). *Leda,* c. 1920. Marble on concrete base; 53.3 x 24.1 cm (not including base). The Art Institute of Chicago, Bequest of Katherine S. Dreier (1953.195).

Louchheim, art critic of the *New York Times,* and Jules Langsner, Los Angeles art critic for *Art News,* mentioned briefly, and in general terms, the negotiations for the disposition of the Arensbergs' collection. Louchheim understood that making modern art accessible to the public would lead to its comprehension and appreciation:

> The fact that every museum in the country which is interested in modern art has been angling, overtly or indirectly, to become future custodian of the collection attests [to] its present-day importance. This attitude also shows how quickly even the most revolutionary movement gains recognition. The recognition may still be reluctant on the part of the public, but it cannot be withheld.[52]

Even though the Art Institute did not obtain the Arensbergs' collection and the Philadelphia Museum of Art became its permanent home, by mounting the first public exhibition of the collection, the Chicago museum paved the way from its private to public recognition. The impact of the exhibition, along with others staged by the museum during these years, on the city of Chicago, the Midwest, and beyond was incalculable. Frank Perls, a Los Angeles art dealer, compared the influence of the exhibition to that of the Armory Show, proposing that it would probably "do as much [for modern art]. . .if not more as [the works] are now more 'readable' and more conclusive."[53] Once again, The Art Institute of Chicago proved itself to be a champion of the cause of modern art.

Appendix

An Interview with Marcel Duchamp at The Art Institute of Chicago, 1949

Peter Pollack, the Art Institute's publicist, wrote to numerous journalists and art critics urging them to "do a story on the [Arensbergs'] collection through a profile on Duchamp,"[54] around the time of the opening of the exhibition. Four accepted Pollack's invitation: Ed Barry (*Chicago Tribune*); Clarence J. Bulliet (*Chicago Daily News*); Lou Spence (*Time*); and Cloyd Head (WMAQ, the NBC-affiliated local radio station). Joining the invited participants were Pollack and Katharine Kuh.

On the morning of October 19, 1949, shortly after Duchamp arrived in Chicago via train from New York, he was "seated in his own gallery" of the Arensberg exhibition "to pose for pictures and be interviewed" (figs. 14, 16, and 17).[55]

In the interview, Duchamp reiterated many of the statements that he made the previous April at the Western Round Table of Modern Art in San Francisco pertaining to artistic impulse; self-criticism by artists; the public reception of art; and the role of critics, collectors, and museums.[56] But whereas the San Francisco symposium was a broader, philosophical inquiry with other participants, the looser format of the Art Institute press conference allowed Duchamp to be more reflective about his own works. He therefore offered explanations on why he ceased painting; on titles to his works and on his use of materials; and on how he presently regarded his oeuvre. Duchamp also surveyed the history of modern art and its future, and expressed his disdain for the increasing commercialism of the art market and his fears about the restraints on artistic freedom.

Although the interview was recorded for radio transmission, it was not aired. The wire recording has not been located. A partial, typed transcript of the interview, with addenda and corrections made by Pollack and others, is in the Archives of The Art Institute of Chicago.

The following edited excerpts are based mostly on the transcript. Because the transcript is incomplete, with apparent breaks in conversation as well as a lack of grammatical and logical syntax, the arrangement of the interview is slightly altered in the excerpts. These also include statements from articles by Barry and Spence, and from a typed version of Head's radio program, "In Our Town," which is in the Archives of the Art Institute.[57] These additions are denoted by an asterisk at the beginning and end of the statement. Additionally, some questions that are lacking in the transcript have been paraphrased (and placed in brackets) in order to retain the conversational flow of the interview. Ellipses (in brackets) denote passages and other words that have been either altered or omitted. The designation "UNIDENTIFIED INTERVIEWER" indicates that the participant posing the question is nameless in the transcript.

DUCHAMP: There's been no listing made of the Arensberg paintings, never entirely. I think this [catalogue *Twentieth-Century Art: From the Louise and Walter Arensberg Collection*] is the first listing of their paintings, isn't it? It is curious, because if you don't do that [recording of information] the minute you get a painting, ten years later you won't recall the date or [other facts] and it is important [for the identification of] the painting later on.

[. . .]

POLLACK: Well, in some cases, Katharine Kuh wrote to artists and refreshed their memory.[58]

DUCHAMP: And the artist sometimes [can't] remember. [. . .Take] the case of a painting shown to an artist who wasn't sure it was his, especially in the case of Matisse. [. . .] It is a great difficulty in the world of art, you know, plagiarism.[59]

[. . .]

BARRY: [. . .Are you painting?]

DUCHAMP: Well, no. *I myself haven't given up painting, I'm just not painting now, but if I have an idea tomorrow I will do it.*[60] *I want to live in whatever way I like. One is not free if one is a painter. The public expects a painter to paint.*[61] [. . .] Most [. . .] painters paint by habit. If they happen to be very well-known painters, okay; everything they do is like a good check, worth lots of money [and] worthy [. . .] of praise. Is it [important] for posterity?—[that's] another question. [Is] every [painting. . .] good enough to keep in museums for [the future?]

[. . .]

[If] anybody wants to paint, I don't object to it. There is no rule about it. [. . .] I don't know whether painting is a profession or should be a profession. A man can be a painter from age twenty to age thirty and then become something else. I don't believe in eternal gifts. A source of inspiration can [. . .] stop [. . .], or at least the desire to paint can stop. It is not essential. A man is not born a genius [to] be one hundred percent like Renoir. *A man can't be a genius all the time. Ideas don't come every day.*[62] [. . .] At least he may be interested in painting [. . .] or [just] having a brush in his hand or smelling the smell of paint, which is most olfactory. One or five of his paintings are real masterpieces after the experts judge [them so], or two centuries later [after] they discover them; but not all of them [can] be marvelous. [. . .For example], a man has a handkerchief one day and a much better handkerchief the next. There is no divinity there. It makes me a little doubtful.

I am not giving up painting. I am not painting. I had the chance to [continue painting for] thirty more years [. . .], but I am not painting. It is because I don't agree with the state of affairs [in] the painting business. [. . .] Even if you can abstract yourself from it, you are [still] in it no matter what you do yourself. The mercantile [status] of painting exists. You will be allowed to sell your paintings or get a dealer to [sell them, but] it has [become] too much [of] a commercial profession for the last one hundred years [. . .], which it didn't used to be. A hundred years ago, there were a few collectors, a few painters, a few critics [. . .], a world of art by itself. Now it is the layman's world. He has the right to say, "This painting is no good. I won't buy it and if I don't buy it, it is a bad painting, [bad] if I decide it is not worth anything." So that makes the whole thing entirely different and uninteresting to me. It is so all over the world. It is even worse in Europe than here. At least people here buy paintings for the sake of buying them and looking at them, while in Europe most collectors, except a few, merely buy to sell again. It is a commercial proposition. It is an investment. Here you have collectors who give their collections to museums. It is still normal [to do so] and [a] bona fide [way of relating to artists and their works]. There are reasons for [the commercialism of art; certainly they are] economic. I don't know them [all. But nothing can] excuse the [current] state of affairs.

UNIDENTIFIED INTERVIEWER: [Collectors] are not buying to hand down from generation to generation?

DUCHAMP: No, [art] has become too popular. Art has become a thing like baseball. Everybody can speak of art. They may, if they want to, but has [this talk] any value? It has [helped to] deteriorate [art]. At least I think it has.

UNIDENTIFIED INTERVIEWER: Was it this state of affairs that persuaded you to drop painting?

DUCHAMP: Well, more or less. I mean I may be lazy, besides.[63] That [. . .] maybe [is] an excuse for the laziness. But after all, it [can take only] five minutes to make a painting if you want. The quicker the better, otherwise one loses the inspiration, [that] subtle thing that comes from the subconscious. You can make three thousand paintings in six months if you want to. So time is an element in our modern life, so many hours, so many dollars. It is ridiculous. It doesn't come into the realm of painting, into the realm of art. [. . .] The problem is [. . .] economics. [. . .] Modern life has taken art [for a] good [ride], for good money [. . .] and deteriorated it or at least distorted it. This doesn't mean that in our time [authentic] works of art will not remain. Surely [some] will, but which ones is another problem. Not necessarily the ones that are in demand today or of interest today; and posterity may be wrong, too. So where are we? I mean, we are not going to discuss art or the definition of art. We cannot do that. It is too far-fetched.

BARRY: Laymen will be asking a great deal within the next few weeks [about the modern art on exhibit from the Arensbergs' collection]. Will you tell us something about that little group in Paris just before the first [World] War, the group that began these innovations? Will you tell us in lay language what that group was seeking; what it revolted against; why it changed the direction of modern art so suddenly?

DUCHAMP: It was not sudden, [. . .]—that is, you can say that modern art starts with Courbet. What we call modern art needs a definition, because if the word "modern" means only the accepted "modern" it means nothing, because [people called themselves] modern in 1649. So there is no point in that [explanation]. As long as we take that terminology, [and] accept the word "modern" [. . .] as [a chronological definition] that [it] means something. Start with Courbet. [. . .From] Courbet and the Impressionists [to] Pointillism, [there was] a definite evolution [from] one [art style to] the other. [After that] every young man, [such as] Matisse when he was young, said "[To] hell with it." If he has some fire in him, he will have to find another [way]. [Certainly influenced and] unconsciously coming out of Pointillism, but still completely different in appearance at least, [were] the Fauves, [who] as early as 1902 or 3 or 4, [. . .] started [out] as a reaction against Pointillism. And then came the ten years of Matisse and the Fauves, [. . .] especially Braque, a new group [emerged], saying, "Well, I want to be something; I want to do something [different]." [This reaction is] true of every generation [. . .] because [painting] is not a totalitarian form of aesthetics [as in the periods in France during the rule of] Louis XIV [. . .], Louis XIII, or Napoleon. [At the time of] Courbet, [there was a conflict that resulted in the decision] that art should be a free affair, and [that] every man has the right to paint as he pleases and it is up to the public to accept or discard it. But at least this [. . .] art is free, not commissioned or ordered. And so it went on from generation to generation, adding more ideas, more theories to it, but the theory only came after. [. . .] A man like Matisse felt like painting as he painted when he was twenty, and the explanation came later as it always does. [. . .] The same thing with the Cubism of Braque, which could be traced back to the last watercolors of Cézanne. When you see the little village of Estaque, or some phase of Braque—1908 or later—and the watercolors of Cézanne, there is a definite relationship there. That doesn't mean anything. Braque was a young man then, and developed something else entirely. There, from that point on [. . .], you [could] add a cube to a line and it becomes more cubistic and things happen. Braque and others made Cubism. You see, it was in the air. And after that came [the theory].

I think the Impressionists had a hard time, a very hard time. In fact, as you all know, [the art dealer Paul] Durand-Ruel, who defended them, neared bankruptcy in 1886 for having tried to make it go and it didn't go, the public didn't respond. *Unless a picture shocks it is nothing—a calendar painting.*[64] [. . .] The fact that you add to a monument, or [to a] stone, that stone should be different, otherwise you are doing [what] Le Brun or Louis XIV were doing. [Then, if an artist] was ordered to make a battle scene, he would make a battle scene; or the portrait painter, [a portrait]. It takes a Clouet, in the case of [his] period, to make it very interesting; and we decided that Clouet was very interesting and we loved Clouet. But is Clouet such an important man? He probably is. But, I mean to say, we made [him so]. In two hundred years, maybe Clouet would be forgotten, the way El Greco [was. . .]. El Greco was forgotten for centuries [until recently]. And all this is another problem, which is much too complex to discuss here.

[UNIDENTIFIED INTERVIEWER: What do you think of the current state of modern art?][65]

DUCHAMP: Modern painting has had one hundred years of life, and that's the end of it. Why not? Let's have a gap for fifty years. There is no reason for going [on]. There will be painters, there will be collectors but in another form.

POLLACK: What form will it be? Do you think it's about due for a transition?

DUCHAMP: Oh, yes, indeed. No transition, but probably a totalitarian form. [Art] is repetitive now.

UNIDENTIFIED INTERVIEWER: Do you believe men like Picasso and Matisse are beginning to change?

DUCHAMP: They are old enough to die in the first place. I mean, we all are [. . .], that's the end.[66]

UNIDENTIFIED INTERVIEWER: You take the intellectual approach [rather than the physical approach to painting]?

DUCHAMP: I take both, but I don't make one more important than the other. I mean to say, the final contact of a painting is not essentially physical or intellectual, because [. . .] intellectual is a bad word, and physical is a bad word. So is something called aesthetics, or art, [which] is another thing that you should define. [. . .] I'll let you define it. I can't.

BARRY: Do you think that modern painting has become too intellectual?

DUCHAMP: No, not at all. It has in some cases, in the way of expression, yes; but this side of intellectualism is uninteresting. Theories of [the] abstract are uninteresting because it is the paintings themselves that count.

[. . .] It [all] has to do with the world as it is today. [. . .] Hitler was the first sign and Stalin is the second sign, and democracy [has also succumbed.] [. . .] We don't want [. . .] more of this free art. We have to control it the way we control everything. Freelance [independent] painting or freelance art will disappear. I'm afraid so. They are already saying it. They accept it and even those [who don't] can kill what exists. [. . .] Modern art had one hundred years [of] life and it exists, it is. It will be in the museums. It will be representative of our period. It's only after this that I don't believe in the existence of it any more, except repetition. *It isn't that modern art is dead, it's just finished, gone.*[67]

[. . .]

Twenty-five years ago, Picasso was a painter in Montmartre, like many of us. He happened to be Picasso later—long after. You could say, today, that if you like a young painter, you like him and he may become a great, great man. But what do you know about it? The last critic is oneself. You think you have done marvelous things when you haven't, and you think that you have done wrong things when you have done something good. You are not the judge—far from it. You are not the critic. You are not a self-critic. You may self-criticize your paintings when you paint, or [you] may say, "I'll put red there, I'll not put a line there." That's not criticizing, it's doing. The intellectual criticism is none of your business [as an artist]. You are the last man to judge anything, even other [artists]—especially the others. A painter is a painter, a poor thing who has an urge to paint, or to do something, and he doesn't know why. He never will know why, and it's of no importance.

[. . .]

But what I was thinking about is showing you these paintings [that are] here [on the wall], my own [paintings]. The light [here] has changed them completely, not only [because of] the way they're lighted and shown, not only [because of] the spacing, but [also] the colors. [Over] the last thirty-six years, I've seen these paintings [on and off] and now I am sure I never saw those colors. I never saw them. All [my] pictures [in] the [Arensbergs'] collection [seem] changed [here]. I mean they are all different than they were in the Arensberg home [in Hollywood, California][68]—there's something very nice about [that]. It gives a new life to the pictures. I wish the Arensbergs could see them [here]. [It] may give them [some new] ideas about the other paintings [in their collection. The Arensbergs] never saw them [in this way. . . .For instance,] there is a little red spot in Matisse's woman's face [of *Mlle. Yvonne Landsberg* (1914) that] I never saw from 1915 on, never saw it, even [at the

FIGURE 16. Duchamp beside *Nude Descending a Staircase, No. 2* (1912; oil on canvas; Philadelphia Museum of Art, Louise and Walter Arensberg Collection), installed in the Duchamp room at the Art Institute's exhibition of the Arensberg Collection, October 19, 1949.

Arensbergs' apartment] in New York.[69] I only saw it today for the first time—a tiny little red spot on the cheek. This is very important, because [now it becomes] an entirely new painting.

[UNIDENTIFIED INTERVIEWER: For most artists, a particular work they have done is often regarded as a watershed, extremely important to their artistic development. Which one of yours do you see as the pivotal painting?]

DUCHAMP: In my case, [*Nude Descending a Staircase, No. 2* (see fig. 16)] was very important, because it was adding intellectual color [. . .], purely cerebral color, which has no equivalent in the light of the sun. [. . .] In other words, [. . .] the title was very important, because it is not only the descriptive title of a nude descending the stairs. It was funny at the time, I remember, it was considered funny.

[UNIDENTIFIED INTERVIEWER: The critics certainly had a field day in the press with the title, such as one newspaper cartoonist calling it "The Rude Descending a Staircase (Rush Hour at the Subway)." Did you also think that the title was funny?]

DUCHAMP: [Yes, it was] funny for me, too, all right. For me too, yes, I had fun finding that title, I had fun. It was great fun. And I said cerebral color because it adds, not in the way of intellectualism, but in the way you [attach] another frame to a painting. If you put a good frame [on] a painting, it will add something to it. It was more than that. The title is enriching.[70] Cerebral, if you want, but not intellectual in the bad sense of the word that people say, "Well, painting is a thing, a physical thing, it should always be physical." For the last fifty years, modern art has made a physical thing of [painting]. I don't believe in that at all. I am delighted that the Surrealists came in time to show [that] there is something [other] than physical painting. I now object to physical [or just purely retinal] painting myself, in general.

[UNIDENTIFIED INTERVIEWER: What is the sex of the nude in the painting?]

DUCHAMP: The sex—feminine.

KUH: Why then "nude" [and] not n-u-e [in the title *Nu descendant un escalier*]?

DUCHAMP: "Nue" would be a cloud. "Nu" is always masculine. In fact, my sister, Suzanne, told me for years that she thought the king and queen were surrounded by flying clouds—swift clouds [in the painting *The King and Queen Surrounded by Swift Nudes / Le Roi et la Reine entourés de nus vites* (1912; see fig. 17)]. She didn't see the spelling ["nus"]. In fact, "nuages-nue" means more [than] the sky. It is a poetic form. Of course, it could be a man. There is no reason [why not, but it is] definitely feminine. In *The King and Queen*, the right-hand side on top is male, the king, and [. . .] the left-hand side is [. . .] female, and that was very important in my painting. [. . .] I felt that the line should express it without using the descriptive form of the body. I am delighted it does.

[. . .]

BARRY: Looking back at your *Nude Descending a Staircase, No. 2*, how do you regard that picture today?

DUCHAMP: I like it very much—more so. I saw it only three times in the last forty years since it was painted. [. . .] I liked it very much in San Francisco, when I saw it just three months ago.[71] It surprised me, because I didn't recall it as brown, or as this or as that—little details. That has been lost in my appreciation of it. Some paintings you don't want to see at all, but this is not the case [with the *Nude*].

[. . .]

[HEAD: I have heard that you consider your painting, *Bride*, a favorite of yours. Why is that?][72]

DUCHAMP: What do I think of [my] painting [*Bride* (fig. 18)]? I love it. [I'll] tell you why. Because that was a real departure from any influence in my case. If you want to be yourself, you say, "Well, this [shows] some influence that I don't like to see." In this case, there [was] no influence. But if you want to see an influence, I'll tell you how it was done. It was Cranach [the Elder] and Böcklin. I was spending three months in Munich when I did it. Already the idea had come into my mind to paint. [. . .] I was painting and I went to the Pinakothek [now Alte Pinakothek] in Munich every day. I love those Cranachs, I love them. Cranach, the old man. The tall nudes. [The] nature and substance of his nudes inspired me for the flesh color, there. At the same time, I went to Bern in Switzerland and studied Böcklin. In Böcklin I found that reaction against physical—what I call retinal—painting, which I already had [the] idea of reacting against, which Impressionism, Pointillism, [and] Fauvism emphasized. I wanted to

FIGURE 17. Duchamp beside *The King and Queen Surrounded by Swift Nudes* (1912; oil on canvas; Philadelphia Museum of Art, Louise and Walter Arensberg Collection), installed in the Duchamp room at the Art Institute's exhibition of the Arensberg Collection, October 19, 1949.

FIGURE 18. Marcel Duchamp. *Bride,* 1912. Oil on canvas; 89.5 x 55 cm. Philadelphia Museum of Art, Louise and Walter Arensberg Collection (50-134-65).

react against retinal painting, and that was my first [try]. Böcklin was the man who gave me the possibility of [doing] it. Looking at [his work], but not copying. Not that I subscribe entirely to Böcklin, but there is something there. He is one of the sources of Surrealism, certainly.

[UNIDENTIFIED INTERVIEWER: Were there other paintings prior to the *Bride* that led to your abandoning of what you call "retinal" or "physical" painting?]

DUCHAMP: First, there was *The Passage from Virgin to Bride* [1912; The Museum of Modern Art, New York]. It was not a physiological passage. It was a passage in my life of painting, one after the other. See that was a pun again, a pun in the title—that idea of the titles. The pun is a poetic element like rhyme. A rhyme is a poem.

BARRY: What about the lumps of sugar [in *Why Not Sneeze Rose Sélavy* (fig. 19)]?

DUCHAMP: The lumps of sugar? That is another question. That's again [. . .] getting off, getting [away from] every usual means of expression, like [using the] brush, canvas stretchers, etc., getting completely out of it, and using anything at all, introducing new materials, etc. And in that case it is again a pun. It is funny that the sugar is not sugar, that the sugar is marble, and this marble is cold, generally, so there is a thermometer to indicate it.[73] It is a mental pun. It is not verbal at all. In fact, if I didn't tell you, you wouldn't see it at all. That's of no importance; either you do or you don't see it. [. . .] As [with] everything in the world, while it is there [. . .] you don't know why, [yet] it attracts you. If it doesn't attract you, nothing is changed. [These] are marble cubes because sugar would never [last]. I knew that if I used sugar, sugar would get dirty and couldn't be cleaned, and in three years it would be destroyed, like [. . .] making a sculpture of soap. In making something solid or [. . .] durable, you [must] think of the preservation of your material. And I introduced the idea of a pun by using marble. And all this goes into a cage, naturally. It is a queer unexpected relation[ship]. An unexpected meeting. That was my idea in [the] "readymades."

FIGURE 19. Marcel Duchamp. *Why Not Sneeze Rose Sélavy?,* 1921. Assisted readymade: painted metal birdcage, marble cubes, thermometer, cuttlebone; 12.4 x 22.2 x 16.2 cm. Philadelphia Museum of Art, Louise and Walter Arensberg Collection (50-134-75).

Notes

MARTINEZ, "A Mixed Reception for Modernism: The 1913 Armory Show at The Art Institute of Chicago," pp. 30–57.

I am grateful to Susan F. Rossen, Executive Director of Publications at the Art Institute, for her limitless assistance and patience in the completion of this essay. I also wish to thank Jack P. Brown, Executive Director of the Ryerson and Burnham Libraries at the Art Institute, for reading the manuscript in various drafts and providing insightful comments. Finally, I wish to thank Robert Cozzolino of the Art Institute Archives for his research assistance.

1. "Director French Flees Deluge of Cubist Art," *Chicago Record-Herald,* Mar. 21, 1913. All of the newspaper articles cited in these notes can be found in the chronological scrapbooks in the Art Institute's Ryerson Library.

2. For more on Eddy's role as an author, collector, and lecturer, see Paul Kruty, "Arthur Jerome Eddy and His Collection: Prelude and Postscript to the Armory Show," *Arts Magazine* 61, 6 (Feb. 1987), pp. 40–47. Rodin's portrait bust of Eddy, as well as the painted portrait by Whistler (see fig. 3 in the present essay), entered the Art Institute's collection in 1931 as part of the Arthur Jerome Eddy Memorial Collection.

3. The Art Institute's most important annual shows featuring American artists were: "The Annual Exhibition of American Painting and Sculpture," which included art by Americans working in Paris; "The Annual Exhibition of Works by Artists of Chicago and Vicinity"; and "The Annual Exhibition of Watercolors by American Artists." The museum often made purchases for its permanent collection from these and other exhibitions.

4. In a letter of Sept. 17, 1908, to Halsey C. Ives of the Museum of Fine Arts, St. Louis, French commented on the exhibition of "the Eight" and stated, "I think it a shame that so fine a man as Davies, who was one of our students, should so sacrifice himself to whimsicalities." Office of the Director, William M. R. French—Letter Books, box 10, vol. 2, 1908, The Art Institute of Chicago Archives (hereafter referred to as AIC Archives).

5. For more on Stieglitz and modernism in America prior to 1913, see Atlanta, High Museum of Art, *The Advent of Modernism: Post-Impressionism and North American Art, 1900–1918,* exh. cat. by William C. Agee, Peter Morrin, and Judith Zilczer (1986), pp. 13–42; and "The Silent Decade: American Art 1900–1910," *Art in America* 61 (July-Aug. 1973), pp. 32–79.

6. See Ann Lee Morgan, "'A Modest Young Man with Theories': Arthur Dove in Chicago, 1912," in Sue Ann Prince, ed., *The Old Guard and the Avant-Garde: Modernism in Chicago, 1910–1940* (Chicago, 1990), pp. 23–37.

7. Amy L. Paulding, "'Futurists' Startle by Hideous Lines," *Chicago Inter-Ocean,* Feb. 27, 1913.

8. "Cast Out Picture; Stir Norwegians," *Chicago Daily Tribune,* Mar. 11, 1913.

9. "Painting Shocks Police Censor," *Chicago Examiner,* Mar. 13, 1913. Fred D. Jackson, owner of the store, was charged with violating a municipal code according to which "no person shall exhibit, sell or offer to sell any picture or other thing whatever of an immoral or scandalous nature." The city ultimately failed to obtain a conviction in court and the city council judiciary committee recommended an ordinance making it "unlawful to display any picture 'representing a person in a nude state' where it can be seen from the street or in a public place frequented by children 'which is not connected with any art or educational exhibition.'" See "Aldermen Pose As Art Censors; Ban On The Nude," *Chicago Inter-Ocean,* Apr. 19, 1913.

10. "When Is Art Art? When Wicked?," *Chicago Daily Tribune,* Mar. 14, 1913; and "Nude In Art O.K. In Proper Place," *New York Telegraph,* Mar. 15, 1913.

11. For a detailed account of the activities of the Association and the planning and showing of the International Exhibition, see Milton W. Brown, *The Story of the Armory Show,* 2nd ed. (New York, 1988).

12. French to Kuhn, Feb. 1, 1912. French—Letter Books, box 15, vol. 1, 1911–12, AIC Archives.

13. The official title for the show was the "Internationale Kunstausstellung des Sonderbundes Westdeutscher Kunstfreunde und Künstler" ("International Art Exhibition of the Federation of West German Art Lovers and Artists").

14. Aldis was introduced to Kuhn by the American sculptor and Association member Jo Davidson. On November 11, Kuhn wrote to his wife that he and Davies had "practically closed a deal with the Chicago Institute to have the show go on there after we close." Walt Kuhn to Vera Kuhn, Nov. 11, 1912. Walt Kuhn Papers, 1901–36, roll D240, Archives of American Art, Smithsonian Institution (hereafter referred to as AAA).

15. French stated his and Hutchinson's role in planning exhibitions in a letter to Sara Hallowell, the Art Institute's European agent, who was based in France. French to Sara Hallowell, Dec. 21, 1912. French—Letter Books, box 16, vol. 1, 1912–13, AIC Archives.

16. As an example of the latitude that individuals were given in their involvement with the Art Institute's exhibitions, the Art Committee's minutes for April 18, 1911, pertaining to Hallowell and her role in obtaining works by American artists in Europe for the annual American Exhibition, state that specific "gentlemen members of the Art Institute, now in Europe, shall be invited to cooperate with Miss Hallowell in obtaining pictures for the exhibition." Board of Trustees Records, Art Committee Minutes, 1902–12, AIC Archives.

17. I am grateful to Mr. Roy E. Porter, the husband of Aldis's granddaughter Mary Cornelia Aldis, for valuable information on Aldis. See also the obituaries for Arthur Aldis in the *Chicago Record-Herald and Examiner* and *Chicago Daily Tribune,* Nov. 24, 1933. In her unpublished autobiography, Alice Gerstenberg, a playwright and participant in activities at "The Compound," described Aldis as "a rather awe-inspiring, large man, with grey whiskers and a self-assured manner of aristocratic bearing. . .and, not being a creative artist himself, he enjoyed by proxy experience mingling with those who were." Alice Gerstenberg, "Come Back With Me," Julia Gerstenberg Papers, Archives and Manuscript collections, Chicago Historical Society, p. 225.

18. The official title of the second Grafton Show was the "Second Post-Impressionist Exhibition." For more on the Grafton shows, see Brown (note 11), pp. 72–73; and Carol A. Nathanson, "The American Reaction to London's First Grafton Show," *Archives of American Art Journal* 25, 3 (1985), pp. 3–10.

19. Aldis asked Ethel L. Coe, an instructor at the School of the Art Institute, who, in 1912–13, was on a leave of absence to study with the painter Joaquin Sorolla y Bastida in Spain, to assemble an exhibition of contemporary Spanish painters. A letter of November 20 from French to Coe once again shows Aldis having taken the initiative to organize an exhibition without consulting anyone at the Art Institute: "Mr. Aldis has returned from Europe and tells me that he wrote to you, and encouraged you to visit Paris to get pictures by Spanish artists resident there." French to Coe, Nov. 20, 1912. French—Letter Books, box 16, vol. 1, 1912–13, AIC Archives.

20. French to Hallowell, Nov. 25, 1912. French—Letter Books, box 16, vol. 1, 1912–13, AIC Archives.

21. French to Townsend, Nov. 19, 1912. French—Letter Books, box 16, vol. 1, 1912–13, AIC Archives.

22. Townsend to French, Nov. 23, 1912. French—Exhibition Correspondence, 1912–14, box 18, AIC Archives.

23. French to Davies, Jan. 14, 1913. French—Letter Books, box 16, vol. 1, 1912–13, AIC Archives. For the correspondence of the Art Institute and the Association regarding the International Exhibition, see French—Letter Books, box 16, vols. 1 and 2, 1912–13; French—Exhibition Correspondence, 1912–14, box 18, AIC Archives; and Armory Show Records, 1912–14, rolls D72–73, AAA.

24. Harriet Monroe, "Art Show Open to Freaks," *Chicago Daily Tribune,* Feb. 17, 1913. For more on the press coverage of the exhibition, see Brown (note 11), pp. 153–86.

25. Aldis to Kuhn, Feb. 17, 1913, Armory Show Records, 1912–14, roll D72, AAA.

26. Kuhn to Aldis, Feb. 19, 1913. Armory Show Records, 1912–14, roll D72, AAA.

27. French to Hutchinson, Feb. 22, 1913, French—Exhibition Correspondence, 1912–14, box 18, AIC Archives. For the full text of French's letter, published here for the first time in its entirety, see Appendix at the end of this essay.

28. Richard R. Brettell and Sue Ann Prince have written that "historians have frequently taken [French's] absence during the show as an indication of his inability to understand the modernists, his blatant uninterest, or his desire to escape confrontation" (Brettell and Prince, "From the Armory Show to the Century of Progress: The Art Institute Assimilates Modernism," in Prince, ed. [note 6], p. 209).

29. Walter Pach, *Queer Thing, Painting* (New York, 1938), pp. 198–99.

30. Peter Morrin, "An Overview: Post-Impressionism and North American Art," in Atlanta, High Museum of Art (note 5), p. 18.

31. Kuhn stated that "Mr. Aldis came from Chicago with a committee to secure the show for the Art Institute." Kuhn, *The Story of the Armory Show* (New York, 1938), p. 19.

32. When presented with the cost of the exhibition, the museum's trustees balked and asked Carpenter to renegotiate the contract so that the Art Institute would be the sole recipient of any profits realized from the sale of catalogues and reproductions. The Association refused to compromise, and the matter ended there. For a copy of the contract and more on the negotiations, see Armory Show Records, 1912–14, roll D72, AAA.

33. French to Coe, Feb. 28, 1913. French—Letter Books, box 16, vol. 2, 1912–13, AIC Archives. In November 1912, after returning from Europe, Kuhn saw the same Scandinavian exhibition in New York and described it as "very tame." Kuhn to Pach, Dec. 12, 1912, Armory Show Records, 1912–14, roll D72, AAA.

34. "I am, as usual, in a pack of trouble about exhibitions. It appears to be settled that we shall bring the great Post-Impressionist show from New York. . . .This is wholly unexpected to me. We need all the room we can get, and I doubt whether the company will be very good for you." French to Pauline Palmer, Mar. 3, 1913. French—Letter Books, box 16, vol. 2, 1912–13, AIC Archives.

35. French wrote to Hutchinson that, "Mr. Lund, the Norwegian artist who came to hang the Scandinavian pictures, thinks so little of Mr. Alexander's works that he is unwilling to talk about them. Alexander, also, I notice is silent about Mr. Lund's work, which in my judgement is, in fact, pretty decomposed." French to Hutchinson, Mar. 5, 1913. French—Letter Books, box 16, vol. 2, 1912–13, AIC Archives. On February 6, 1913, Gutzon Borglum, vice president of the Association and chairman of its sculpture committee, realizing that he was powerless in the face of Davies's strong executive control, resigned from the Association. See Brown (note 11), pp. 99–106.

36. Aldis to Newton H. Carpenter, Mar. 5, 1913. French—Exhibition Correspondence, 1912–14, box 18, AIC Archives.

37. "Hit Mud With Brick; Result, Cubist Art," *Chicago Inter-Ocean,* Mar. 9, 1913.

38. French to Davies, Mar. 6, 1913. French—Letter Books, box 16, vol. 2, 1912–13, AIC Archives.

39. Davies to French, Mar. 13, 1913. Armory Show Records, 1912–14, roll D72, AAA.

40. Eddy to Davies, Mar. 15, 1913. Armory Show Records, 1912–14, roll D72, AAA. Among Eddy's purchases in New York were Derain's *Forest at Martigues,* Duchamp's *King and Queen Surrounded by Swift Nudes* and *Portrait of Chess Players,* Gleizes's *Man on Balcony,* Picabia's *Dances at the Spring,* Villon's *Young Girl,* and Vlaminck's *Village (Rueil).* Eddy's purchases from both the New York and Chicago showings totaled eighteen paintings and seven lithographs at a cost of $4,888.50, making him the second largest buyer, after John Quinn, the Association's legal advisor, from the International Exhibition. For more on purchases from the exhibition, see Brown (note 11), pp. 119–32.

41. "For the benefit of those stupid Chicagoans whose souls cannot open themselves and receive the soul expression of the cubist artists and sculptors, a special volume of explanatory literature has been sent to the Art Institute. It was written by Miss Gertrude Stein of Paris, first cubist writer in the world" ("Cubist Art Is Explained Clearly by a Post-Impressionist Writer," *Chicago Inter-Ocean,* Mar. 21, 1913). Grace Gassette, a Chicago painter, offered

for the Chicago showing of the International Exhibition her relatively straightforward portrait of Gertrude Stein, which French gladly accepted. It was even listed in the exhibition catalogue under no. 148½. Apparently, the Association vetoed this addition, for after the show French apologized to Gassette for the exclusion of her painting. See French to Gassette, June 7, 1913. French—Letter Books, box 16, vol. 2, 1912–13, AIC Archives.

42. See Kuhn to Vera Kuhn, Mar. 23, 1913. Walt Kuhn Papers, 1901–36, roll D240, AAA. Of the six hundred and thirty-four works exhibited, three hundred and twelve were oil paintings, fifty-seven were watercolors, one hundred twenty were prints, one hundred fifteen were drawings, and thirty were sculptures. The Art Institute of Chicago, *Thirty-Fourth Annual Report for the Year 1912–13,* p. 89. Brown (note 11), p. 107, estimated that approximately one thousand three hundred works were displayed in New York.

43. Board of Trustees Records, Trustee Minutes, vol. 4, pp. 253–54, AIC Archives. The American artist William Zorach, who showed two works in the International Exhibition, described the Henri as "the most realistic and nudist nude I ever saw" (Utica, N.Y., Munson-Williams-Proctor Institute, *1913 Armory Show 50th Anniversary Exhibition 1963*, exh. cat. [New York, 1963], p. 94).

44. Childe Hassam, David Milne, and Sydney Dale Shaw had the distinction of being represented in both the International Exhibition and "The Annual Exhibition of Watercolors by American Artists."

45. Carpenter to Hutchinson, Mar. 25, 1913. French—Exhibition Correspondence, 1912–14, box 18, AIC Archives.

46. Burkholder to French, Mar. 27, 1913. French—Letter Books, box 16, vol. 2, 1912–13, AIC Archives.

47. See Brown (note 11), pp. 203–08.

48. Joan Candoer, *Chicago Examiner,* Mar. 28, 1913.

49. *Chicago Daily Tribune,* Mar. 24, 1913.

50. See Brown (note 11), p. 208.

51. "President Wilson a Cubist? Sure! Art Collector Says," *Chicago Daily Tribune,* Apr. 4, 1913.

52. "Chicago Artist Starts Revolt," *Chicago Daily Tribune,* Mar. 26, 1913.

53. Kuhn to Vera Kuhn, Mar. 25, 1913. Walt Kuhn Papers, 1901–36, roll D240, AAA.

54. "Fair Play for Insurgent Art," *Chicago Evening Post,* Mar. 24, 1913.

55. See review by Herman Landon in the *Chicago Record-Herald,* Mar. 23, 1913. An early press release from the Association stated that artists representing the Italian Futurist movement would be included in the exhibition. The Futurists purportedly declined to participate in the show because they would not be allowed to exhibit as a group. See Brown (note 11), p. 79.

56. Otto Nohn Behterr, "An Attentive Survey of the Cubists," *Chicago Record-Herald,* Mar. 30, 1913; and "Cubist Art Severs Friendships, Institute Directors Are Divided," *Chicago Examiner,* Mar. 28, 1913.

57. See review by George B. Zug, *Chicago Inter-Ocean,* Mar. 30, 1913.

58. "May Bar Youngsters From Cubists' Show," *Chicago Record-Herald,* Mar. 27, 1913.

59. See Kuhn to Vera Kuhn, Mar. [?], 1913. Walt Kuhn Papers, 1901–36, roll D240, AAA.

60. "Futurist Art Included in State Vice Inquiry," *Chicago Daily Journal,* Apr. 1, 1913. Brown (note 11), pp. 206–07, stated that it was actually Coan's sister, Mrs. Maud J. Coan Josephare, who visited the exhibition and apprised her brother of its contents.

61. Burkholder to French, Apr. 2, 1913. French—Letter Books, box 16, vol. 2, 1912–13, AIC Archives.

62. See Kruty (note 2), p. 47 n. 40.

63. Sherwood Anderson, *Sherwood Anderson's Memoirs,* ed. Paul Rosenfeld (New York, 1942), p. 234.

64. Floyd Dell, "The Portrait of Murray Swift," Floyd Dell Papers, Collection of Modern Manuscripts, Newberry Library, Chicago. In his memoirs, Dell wrote that "modern art was as new to all except a few people in America as it was to me. Post-Impressionism exploded like a bombshell within the minds of everybody who could be said to have minds. For Americans it could not be merely an aesthetic experience; it was an emotional experience which led to a philosophical and moral reevaluation of life." Idem, *Homecoming (An Autobiography of Floyd Dell)* (New York, 1953), p. 238.

65. See Ed Garman, *The Art of Raymond Jonson, Painter* (Albuquerque, 1976), pp. 23–24; and Mark Haworth-Booth, *E. McKnight Kauffer: A Designer and His Public* (London, 1979), pp. 13–14.

66. For more on Dawson's development as a modernist painter, see Kenneth R. Hey, "Manierre Dawson: A Fix on the Phantoms of the Imagination," *Archives of American Art Journal* 14, 4 (1974), pp. 7–12; and Mary Gedo, "Modernizing the Masters: Manierre Dawson's Cubist Transliterations," *Arts Magazine* 55, 8 (Apr. 1981), pp. 135–45.

67. The Dawson journal entries quoted in this article may all be found in the Manierre Dawson Journal, 1908–22, roll 64, AAA.

68. The Duchamp painting that Dawson purchased has since been renamed *Sad Young Man on a Train.* See Brown (note 11), pp. 264 and 318.

69. "Parody on Cubists," *Chicago Record-Herald,* Mar. 27, 1913.

70. "'Cliff Dwellers' Satirize the Cubist Art in Pointed Caricatures," *Chicago Examiner,* Apr. 2, 1913.

71. Kuhn to Vera Kuhn, Mar. 30, 1913. Walt Kuhn Papers, 1901–36, roll D240, AAA.

72. Brown (note 11), p. 209. There was at least one School faculty member who was sympathetic to the modernists, and that was Dudley Crafts Watson. As early as 1911, Watson had encouraged Dawson in his experiments with abstraction. Watson lectured on the International Exhibition and one can assume that his attitude toward the show was positive because, by December 1913, he had accepted the position of director of the Milwaukee Art Society, for

which he arranged, as one of his first shows, "Exhibition of Paintings and Sculpture in 'The Modern Spirit,'" which displayed works by American modernists such as Dawson. Watson joined the staff of the Art Institute again as a lecturer in 1924.

73. Kuhn to Pach, Apr. 5, 1913. Armory Show Records, 1912–14, roll D72, AAA.

74. Burkholder to French, Apr. 8, 1913. French—Letter Books, box 16, vol. 2, 1912–13, AIC Archives.

75. Bennett to French, Apr. 10, 1913. French—Exhibition Correspondence, 1912–14, box 18, AIC Archives.

76. Carpenter to French, Apr. 7, 1913. French—Exhibition Correspondence, 1912–14, box 18, AIC Archives.

77. "Cubist Art Exhibit Ends 'at the Stake,'" *Chicago Record-Herald,* Apr. 17, 1913. Oddly enough, that same evening the students staged a protest against censorship with a mock trial of Chabas's *September Morn.*

78. "Students Wreak Vengeance Upon Cubist Designs," *Chicago Evening Post,* Apr. 17, 1913.

79. "Cubist Art Exhibit Ends 'at the Stake'" (note 77).

80. For more on the International Exhibition in Boston, see Brown (note 11), pp. 215–22; and Garnett McCoy, "The Post Impressionist Bomb," *Archives of American Art Journal* 20, 1 (1980), pp. 13–17.

81. Carpenter to Kuhn, Apr. 21, 1913. Armory Show Records, 1912–14, roll D72, AAA.

82. "Exhibition of Modern Art," *Bulletin of The Art Institute of Chicago* 6, 4 (Apr. 1913), p. 51.

83. French to Ryerson, May 10, 1913. French—Letter Books, box 16, vol. 2, 1912–13, AIC Archives. For French's comments regarding the effect of the exhibition on the city's art students, see "Director French Fears Cubists' Chicago Effect," *Chicago Examiner,* Apr. 27, 1913.

84. The Art Institute of Chicago, *Thirty-Fourth Annual Report For the Year 1912–13;* "The International Exhibition of Modern Art," *Bulletin of The Art Institute of Chicago* 7, 1 (July 1913), p. 4.

85. Pach to Robert Koehler, Apr. 26, 1913. Armory Show Records, 1912–14, roll D72, AAA. Koehler, director of the art school of the Minneapolis Society of Fine Arts, who saw the International Exhibition in Chicago, exchanged letters commenting upon the lack of acceptance of the new art among Chicago's artists.

86. While Harriet Monroe confessed to Dawson that "she didn't understand the new things and that she hadn't seen anything good in the Armory Show," she did purchase one Redon lithograph. Mary Aldis purchased three other lithographs by Redon; George F. Porter bought paintings by James Pryde, Jack Yeats, and a screen by Robert Chanler. The Art Institute's Friends of American Art acquired a portrait by Mary Foote for the museum's collection. While in Chicago, Kuhn had tried, apparently in vain, to sell a work by Gauguin to Emily Crane Chadbourne, a Chicagoan and part-time resident of Paris, as well as an acquaintance of Gertrude Stein. Chadbourne lent four works on paper by Gauguin (see fig. 8 in the present essay) and a pastel by Redon to the International Exhibition. See Kuhn to Vera Kuhn, Mar. 30, 1913. Walt Kuhn Papers, 1901–36, roll D240, AAA. For more purchases from the exhibition in Chicago, see Brown (note 11), p. 213.

87. See Burkholder to Eddy, Apr. 19, 1913. French—Letter Books, box 16, vol. 2, 1912–13, AIC Archives. For more on Eddy's activities following the International Exhibition, see Kruty (note 2), pp. 44–45.

88. For more on the assimilation of modernism into American museum collections, see Judith Zilczer, "The Dissemination of Post-Impressionism in North America: 1905–1918," in Atlanta, High Museum of Art (note 5), pp. 34–39.

89. In 1922, Aldis lobbied the trustees to exhibit Eddy's collection so as to get a better idea of how it would look in the museum. Aldis hoped that the trustees would want to acquire some of the works, but the issue was never voted upon. Office of the Director, Robert B. Harshe—Correspondence, box 1, 1921–22, folder 8, AIC Archives.

90. For more information on the Art Institute and its acquisitions of modern art, see Brettell and Prince (note 28), pp. 209–25.

91. The Art Institute of Chicago, *Exhibition of Modern Paintings by Albert Bloch of Munich,* exh. cat. (1915), p. 10.

SMITH, "The Nervous Profession: Daniel Catton Rich and The Art Institute of Chicago, 1927–1958," pp. 58–79.

I would like to acknowledge Penelope Rich Jarchow for providing me with many photographs of her father, as well as biographical information about his childhood. Special thanks go to Katharine Kuh for her insight and encouragement from the time I first began working on this project. I also wish to thank Susan F. Rossen, Executive Director of Publications at the Art Institute, and Jack P. Brown, Executive Director of the Ryerson and Burnham Libraries at the Art Institute, for their careful readings of the manuscript.

1. Ernest L. Heitkamp, "Art Institute's New Chief, Just 34, Tells His Policies," *Chicago American,* May 12, 1938.

2. Ibid.

3. Much of the biographical material used in this article is drawn from an oral history that was conducted with Rich by Paul Cummings on November 11 and 23, 1970, in New York City, under the auspices of the Archives of American Art, Smithsonian Institution.

4. See, in this issue, Andrew Martinez, "A Mixed Reception for Modernism: The 1913 Armory Show at The Art Institute of Chicago," pp. 30–57.

5. See, in this issue, Naomi Sawelson-Gorse, "The Art Institute of Chicago and the Arensberg Collection," pp. 80–101.

6. Agnes Mongan, "The Heavenly Twins," *Apollo* 196 (June 1978), pp. 477–79.

7. C. J. Bulliet, "Art World Mourns Harshe, Builder of Great Collections," *Chicago Daily News,* Jan. 11, 1938.

8. The Arts Club of Chicago was founded in 1916 to foster the understanding of art in this city by sponsoring exhibitions and other programs. From its beginning, the organization showed a propensity for supporting the avant-garde. The Arts Club held shows at the Art Institute from 1922 until 1927, including exhibitions of the work of Picasso (1923 and 1924), Braque (1924), Elie Nadelman (1925), and Gaston Lachaise (1926). For a history of the Arts Club's early years, see Arts Club of Chicago, *Portrait of an Era: Rue Winterbotham Carpenter and the Arts Club of Chicago,* exh. cat. (1986). See also Richard R. Brettell and Sue Ann Prince, "From the Armory Show to the Century of Progress: The Art Institute Assimilates Modernism," in Prince, ed., *The Old Guard and the Avant-Garde: Modernism in Chicago, 1910–1940* (Chicago, 1990), pp. 209–25.

9. When this painting was accessioned in 1926, it was entitled *Un Dimanche à La Grande Jatte.*

10. Rich interview (note 3).

11. Barr remained at The Museum of Modern Art in various capacities until his retirement in 1967. In a special issue of *The New Criterion* (Summer 1987), Rona Roob and Barr's widow, Margaret Scolari Barr, provided a detailed chronology of the years 1902–44. For a fuller discussion of Barr's life, see Alice Goldfarb Marquis, *Alfred H. Barr, Jr., Missionary for the Modern* (Chicago and New York, 1989).

After seventeen years as director of the Wadsworth Atheneum, Austin left in 1944. In 1946, he became the first director of the Ringling Museum of Art, Sarasota, Fla., staying until his premature death in 1957. See Nicholas Fox Weber, *Patron Saints: Five Rebels Who Opened America to a New Art, 1928–1943* (New York, 1992).

12. Daniel Catton Rich, "Letter to Paul" (paper delivered at the American Federation of Arts Convention in Des Moines, Iowa, on Oct. 14, 1955). Office of the Director, Daniel Catton Rich, Office Files—Lectures and Articles, box 86, The Art Institute of Chicago Archives (hereafter referred to as AIC Archives).

13. Among the books and catalogues Rich wrote, see particularly *Cézanne: Paintings, Watercolors, and Drawings,* exh. cat. (Chicago, 1952); *Edgar Hilaire Germain Degas* (New York, 1951); *Henri Rousseau,* exh. cat. (New York, 1941); and *Seurat, Paintings and Drawings,* exh. cat. (Chicago, 1958).

14. The Art Institute of Chicago, *Report for the Year 1930,* p. 33.

15. The Art Institute of Chicago, *The Arthur Jerome Eddy Collection of Modern Paintings and Sculpture,* exh. cat. (1931).

16. The Art Institute of Chicago, *The Mrs. L. L. Coburn Collection of Modern Paintings and Watercolors,* exh. cat. (1932).

17. In a letter to Frederic Bartlett, Harshe outlined his plan to rehang the permanent collection chronologically. He wrote that "the Trustees. . .felt that to go back to the original system of hanging. . .would be distinctly retrogressive." Robert Harshe to Frederic Bartlett, July 15, 1933, Registrar Collection Records, box 1, Birch-Bartlett file, AIC Archives. See also Brettell and Prince (note 8), pp. 222–23.

18. In a November 1, 1933, article in the *Chicago Daily News,* Chauncey McCormick, chairman of the Fine Arts Committee, acknowledged that the "show could not have taken place without Dr. Harshe and Daniel Catton Rich."

19. The Art Institute of Chicago, *Catalogue of a Century of Progress Exhibition of Paintings and Sculpture: Lent from American Collections,* exh. cat. (1933).

20. Eleanor Jewett, "Catalogue of A Century of Progress Art Exhibit at Institute Wins Hearty Praise of Visitors," *Chicago Tribune,* July 9, 1933.

21. Daniel Catton Rich, *Seurat and the Evolution of "La Grande Jatte"* (Chicago, 1935).

22. Susan F. Rossen, "Foreword," *The Art Institute of Chicago Museum Studies* 14, 2 (1989), p. 112. This issue of the museum's journal is devoted to the *Grande Jatte.*

23. Jere Abbott to Daniel Catton Rich, Jan. 11, 1938. Museum Staff Subject files—Robert Harshe, AIC Archives.

24. Joseph Winterbotham to Daniel Catton Rich, Feb. 28, 1938. Museum Staff Subject files—Robert Harshe, AIC Archives.

25. The Art Institute of Chicago, *Retrospective Exhibition of Robert B. Harshe,* exh. cat. (1938).

26. According to critic C. J. Bulliet, the death of Harshe reignited the battle between the progressive and conservative factions of the museum's board. Potter Palmer II reportedly calmed matters down and, after Rich was given the directorship, promised to see him "through troubles that might be immediately ahead." See C. J. Bulliet, "Artless Comment on the Seven Arts," *Chicago Daily News* (Nov. 1943).

27. The Art Institute of Chicago, *Annual Report for the Year 1938,* pp. 8–9.

28. Ibid., p. 9.

29. Rich, "Letter to Paul" (note 12).

30. *Annual Report for the Year 1938* (note 27), p. 26.

31. Susan F. Rossen and Charlotte Moser, "Primer for Seeing: The Gallery of Art Interpretation and Katharine Kuh's Crusade for Modernism in Chicago," *The Art Institute of Chicago Museum Studies* 16, 1 (Spring 1990), p. 11.

32. See *Museum News* 23 (Sept. 1, 1945–Apr. 15, 1946) and 24 (May 15, 1946). Rich's paper, "Special Exhibitions," appears in the issue of Oct. 1, 1945, pp. 6–8.

33. See Office of the Director, Daniel Catton Rich, Office Files—Television Department, 1957, box 48, AIC Archives.

34. Rich interview (note 3).

35. The Art Institute of Chicago, *Annual Report for the Year 1939,* p. 5.

36. Frederick Sweet, *Miss Mary Cassatt, Impressionist from Pennsylvania* (Norman, Okla., 1966).

37. In a further effort to popularize the museum, Rich announced plans in 1944 to open a series of small, branch museums, to be scattered throughout Chicago neighborhoods, that would offer "art exhibits in smaller, friendlier, and close-to-home galleries" for people who might have been intimidated by the Art Institute itself.

These branch museums, however, were never built. See "Take Art to the People," *Pasadena Californian Post,* Aug. 13, 1944.

38. Rich interview (note 3).

39. Ibid.

40. At that time, The Museum of Modern Art was in charge of selecting which institution would organize the United States Pavilion. Katharine Kuh's close friend, the Chicago collector Arnold Maremont, offered to underwrite the cost of the exhibition if Kuh were allowed to curate it. Kuh organized "American Artists Paint the City," which was installed in Venice during the summer of 1956, and was later shown in Chicago as the "62nd Annual Exhibition of American Painting and Sculpture" (Jan. 17–Mar. 3, 1957).

41. In March and May 1944, over two hundred fifty paintings from the Art Institute's collection were auctioned by Parke-Bernet Galleries, New York. See New York, Parke-Bernet Galleries, *Notable Paintings Including an Important Portrait by Manet and Works by Monet, Gauguin, Pissarro, Corot, Cazin, Inness and the Earlier Masters Ysenbrant, Hobbema, Cuyp, and Others: Property of a Mid-Western Educational Institution,* pt. 1 (Mar. 2, 1944); and idem, *Notable Paintings by Modern and Barbizon Artists and Old Masters including Monet, Degas, Derain, Corot, Cazin, Inness, Bellows, Il Francia, Lucas Cranach, Nattier, Lawrence, Romney and Other Artists: Property of a Mid-Western Educational Institution,* 2nd and final pt. (May 4, 1944).

42. Rich interview (note 3).

43. Daniel Catton Rich, "Chauncey McCormick: Some Recollections," *The Art Institute of Chicago Quarterly* 48, 4 (Nov. 15, 1954), pp. 62–64.

44. Chester Dale was a notoriously temperamental and difficult man. For a discussion of his character and his involvement with the National Gallery, see Paul Mellon, *Reflections in a Silver Spoon* (New York, 1992), pp. 306–10.

45. Roxana Robinson, *Georgia O'Keeffe: A Life* (New York, 1989), p. 329.

46. Laurie Lisle, *Portrait of the Artist: A Biography of Georgia O'Keeffe* (Albuquerque, 1986), p. 178.

47. Robinson (note 45), p. 453.

48. In the AIC Archives, there are dozens of letters that O'Keeffe wrote to Rich from 1944 to 1958. See Office of the Director, Daniel Catton Rich—Office Files, AIC Archives.

49. For correspondence, as well as details on accompanying programs, see Office of the Director, Daniel Catton Rich, Exhibition Records—Masterpieces of English Painting, box 66, AIC Archives.

50. The scope of Sweet's and Kuh's research is evident in their travel notes. See Department of Painting and Sculpture, Exhibition records—58th Annual Exhibition of American Painting and Sculpture, 1947, box 5, AIC Archives.

51. The Art Institute of Chicago, *Catalogue of the 58th Annual Exhibition of American Painting and Sculpture,* exh. cat. (1947).

52. Rough draft of interview with Alfred Barr, conducted by Peter Pollack. Department of Painting and Sculpture, Exhibition records—58th Annual Exhibition of American painting and sculpture, 1947, box 5, AIC Archives. It is unclear under what circumstances this interview took place.

53. Daniel Catton Rich, "Freedom of the Brush," *Atlantic Monthly,* 181, 1 (Feb., 1948), p. 51.

54. Walter Trohan, "Reds Corrupt American Art, House Is Told," *Chicago Tribune,* Aug. 17, 1949.

55. Rich did not enjoy administrative work, nor was he particularly astute at it. In 1956, in an effort to relieve Rich of some of the administrative duties, the trustees hired Allan McNab as assistant director (see, in this essay, fig. 23). McNab had been director of the Lowe Gallery at the University of Miami, as well as an advisor to the National Museum in Havana, Cuba. Upon his arrival, he undertook much of the responsibility for overseeing renovation and building projects.

56. Among Rich's many interests outside the museum, his involvement with *Poetry* magazine was particularly meaningful to him. Rich served as president of the board of *Poetry* from 1951 until 1953. He had published his own poetry in the magazine during the late 1920s and early 1930s. His wife worked for *Poetry* for several years as an editor and translator. According to Joseph Parisi, the current *Poetry* editor, "The period 1950–1955 marks a high point in the history of the magazine." See Parisi, *Poetry: An American Institution* (Chicago, 1980), p. 8.

57. For a discussion of the legal problems encountered by the museum before constructing the B. F. Ferguson Memorial Building, see Robert Bruegmann, "The Art Institute Expands: Challenges of Mid-Century," *The Art Institute of Chicago Museum Studies* 14, 1 (1988), pp. 57–81.

58. Rich, "Letter to Paul" (note 12).

59. Office of the Director, Daniel Catton Rich, Exhibition Records—Seurat Paintings and Drawings, box 79, AIC Archives.

60. "Churchill Amateur, Art Institute Decides," *Chicago Tribune,* Apr. 22, 1958.

61. Gwen Morgan, "British Attack Rich for Slam at Churchill," *Chicago Tribune,* Apr. 24, 1958.

62. Doris Lane Butler, "Loss of Art Institute Chief Fresh Cultural Blow to City," *Chicago Daily News,* Apr. 29, 1958.

63. Interview between Leigh Block and Herman Kogan, June 20–21, 1985. Transcript in AIC Archives.

SAWELSON-GORSE, "The Art Institute of Chicago and the Arensberg Collection," pp. 80–101.

My deepest appreciation goes to Katharine Kuh, who consented to interviews (November 14 and 29, and December 20, 1989), answered queries on the telephone and in letters, and granted me access to her interview conducted by Avis Berman for the Archives of American Art. Her willingness to review with me her relationship with the Arensbergs and Duchamp, no matter how painful the memories, or how the factual information I brought to her attention revised her previous assessments, came from, as she continually told me, her desire to "put the record straight." My indebtedness to Elizabeth S. Wrigley, president of the Francis Bacon Foundation, who was hired as Walter Arensberg's research assistant in 1944, is incalculable. Off and on since 1980, she has shared with me innumerable stories about the Arensbergs, some of which are told here. To these two eyewitnesses, this article is fondly dedicated.

I would also like to thank Alexina Duchamp for permission to quote from Duchamp's letters and to publish the Art Institute interview with Duchamp (see Appendix in the present essay). I wish to acknowledge the assistance of John W. Smith and Andrew Martinez, Archives of the Art Institute; Marge Kline, Philadelphia Museum of Art; Richard A. Born, Curator, The David and Alfred Smart Museum of Art, University of Chicago; Rebecca E. Lawton, Curator of Collections, Art Gallery, Vassar College; Judy Throm, Archives of American Art, Smithsonian Institution; Christina Houssian; Catherine C. Bock, The School of The Art Institute of Chicago; George L. Gorse and Richard Harrison, Pomona College; and the staff of the Harry S. Truman Presidential Library. A special note of thanks goes to Susan F. Rossen, Executive Director of Publications at the Art Institute, for her continual encouragement and support.

The archival documents cited in the notes are housed in the Archives of American Art, Smithsonian Institution (referred to here as AAA); the Archives of The Art Institute of Chicago (referred to as AIC Archives); the Arensberg Archives, Francis Bacon Library, Claremont, Calif. (referred to as FBL); the Arensberg Archives, Philadelphia Museum of Art (referred to as PMA); and the Yale Collection of American Literature, Beinecke Rare Book and Manuscript Library, Yale University (referred to as Beinecke). Newspaper articles designated AIC Ryerson can be found in the chronological scrapbooks housed in the Art Institute's Ryerson Library.

All quotations of Louise Stevens Arensberg and Walter Conrad Arensberg are copyright © 1993 The Francis Bacon Foundation. No part of these writings can be further published or duplicated in any form without the written consent of the Francis Bacon Foundation.

1. Although 198 works are listed in the catalogue (The Art Institute of Chicago, *Twentieth-Century Art: From the Louise and Walter Arensberg Collection,* exh. cat. [1949]), the actual number of objects was 196. Two paintings—one by Georges Braque, the other by Morton Schamberg—had images on the front and back; see idem, p. 26, no. 31a-b (for Braque's *Still Life* and *The Table*), and p. 32, no. 197a-b (for Schamberg's *Mechanical Abstraction* and *Landscape*).

2. These included works by Duchamp (three of the four in the 1913 show); Gleizes's *Man on Balcony*; La Fresnaye's *Landscape*; Picabia's *Dances at the Spring*; Picasso's *Landscape*; and Villon's *Young Girl.* Additionally, fifteen artists who had works in the 1913 show were represented by other objects in the 1949 exhibition: Archipenko, Brancusi, Braque, Cézanne, Delaunay, Derain, Duchamp-Villon, Kandinsky, Léger, Matisse, Renoir, Rouault, Rousseau, Schamberg, and Sheeler.

3. These were Duchamp's *Portrait of Chess Players,* Gleizes's *Man on Balcony*, Picabia's *Dances at the Spring*, and Villon's *Young Girl.* The Eddy collection was shown at the Art Institute on September 19–October 22, 1922, and December 22, 1931–January 17, 1932. On Eddy, his collection, and his association with the museum, see Paul Kruty, "Arthur Jerome Eddy and His Collection: Prelude and Postscript to the Armory Show," *Arts Magazine* 61, 6 (Feb. 1987), pp. 40–47; and, in this issue, Andrew Martinez, "A Mixed Reception for Modernism: The 1913 Armory Show at The Art Institute of Chicago," pp. 30–57.

4. Still, today, there is little published information about the Arensbergs. No biography exists, although there have been several articles and parts of books that discuss various aspects of their lives: see, for instance, Naomi Sawelson-Gorse, "Hollywood Conversations: Duchamp and the Arensbergs," in *West Coast Duchamp,* ed. Bonnie Clearwater (Miami Beach, 1991), pp. 24–45; Francis M. Naumann, "Walter Conrad Arensberg: Poet, Patron, and Participant in the New York Avant-Garde, 1915–20," *Philadelphia Museum of Art Bulletin* 76 (1980), pp. 2–32; Anne d'Harnoncourt, "A. E. Gallatin and the Arensbergs: Pioneer Collectors of Twentieth-Century Art," *Apollo* 100 (1974), pp. 52–61; and Fiske Kimball, "Cubism and the Arensbergs," *Art News* 53, 7 (1954), pp. 117–22, 174–78. For early biographical information on Louise Arensberg, see Naomi Sawelson-Gorse's forthcoming dissertation, "Marcel Duchamp's 'Silent Guard': A Critical Biography of Louise and Walter Arensberg," for the University of California, Santa Barbara.

5. These include *The Burial of Francis Bacon and His Mother at Lichfield* (1924); *The Baconian Keys* (1928); *The Shakespearian Mystery* (1928); *The Magic Ring of Francis Bacon* (1929); *Francis Bacon, William Butts, and the Pagets of Beaudesert* (1929). His earlier works, printed by established publishers, were: *The Cryptography of Dante* (New York, 1921); *The Cryptography of Shakespeare, Part I* (Los Angeles, 1922); and *The Secret Grave of Francis Bacon at Lichfield* (San Francisco, 1923).

6. Katharine Kuh, telephone conversation with the author, May 8, 1991.

7. Indeed, one critic called them "quite mad"; see Henry McBride, "The Walter Arensbergs," in *The Flow of Art: Essays and Criticisms of Henry McBride,* ed. Daniel Catton Rich (New York, 1975), p. 156; first published as "Modern Forms" in *The Dial* 69 (July 1920), p. 61.

8. Statement by William M. Ivins, Jr., a former Harvard classmate of Walter's, cited in Kimball, "Cubism and the Arensbergs" (note 4), p. 120, excerpted from a letter from Ivins to Kimball, Mar. 15, 1954; the original document is in the Fiske Kimball Papers, Department of Twentieth-Century Art, Philadelphia Museum of Art.

9. Katharine Kuh, "Walter Arensberg and Marcel Duchamp," *The Open Eye: In Pursuit of Art* (New York, 1971), p. 60.

10. The document, addressed to an unknown friend (perhaps Helen Scholz), is in the FBL. The complete text of the card reads: "Bestes Lämmchen [Little lambchop]. Sehen wir so aus [How are you]. This is almost the mildest atrocity in the exhibition & most of the paintings are weird & grotesque & simply frightful too. Let me know before you come[.] We must all 3 have a theater & dinner brot [meal]. I'm working hard wallied [*sic*] from 9 to 4:30 today dinner excluded & yesterday all day. Am not sehr [sure] yet but guess will be in a.m. I love it [New York] & its just like a german Jahrmarkt [annual festival] all the time."

11. Their intense association continued even after Duchamp went back to France in the 1920s (he returned to New York at the outbreak of World War II) and the Arensbergs moved to California in 1927. Duchamp and the Arensbergs only saw each other four times after the couple settled in Hollywood (once in 1936, twice in 1949, and, for the last time, in 1950). For discussions of Duchamp with

the Arensbergs from the 1920s until their deaths, see Sawelson-Gorse, "Hollywood Conversations" (note 4); and idem, "'For the want of a nail': The Disposition of the Louise and Walter Arensberg Collection" (M.A. thesis, University of California, Riverside, 1987).

12. Letter from Duchamp to Walter Pach, Sept. 28, 1937, Walter Pach Papers, roll 4218, frames 569–70, AAA; English translation in "*Amicalement, Marcel*: Fourteen Letters from Marcel Duchamp to Walter Pach," ed. Francis M. Naumann, *Archives of American Art Journal* 29, 3–4 (1989), p. 46.

13. On these aspects of Duchamp's association with the Arensbergs, see Sawelson-Gorse, "'For the want of a nail'" (note 11). For other discussions of Duchamp's works in the Arensbergs' collection, see Katharine Kuh, "Marcel Duchamp," in *Twentieth-Century Art* (note 1), pp. 11–18; and James Thrall Soby, "Marcel Duchamp in the Arensberg Collection," *View* 5, 1 (1945), pp. 11–12.

14. Letter from Walter Arensberg to Duchamp, Jan. 11, 1945, FBL.

15. Statement by Henry Hopkins at the West Coast Duchamp Symposium, Dec. 8, 1990, cited in Clearwater, ed. (note 4), p. 119.

16. Duchamp, press interview at the Art Institute, Oct. 19, 1949, Public Relations files, AIC Archives; for the edited text of this interview, see Appendix to the present essay. Duchamp further commented that the installation's "general effect was that all the paintings had been cleaned and in the case of [my 1911 painting *Portrait (Dulcinea)*], hung in [the Arensbergs'] dining room, all the colors stood out as though the painting had been painted yesterday" (letter from Duchamp to the Arensbergs, Oct. 21, 1949, FBL). In fact, shortly before the Chicago exhibition, Duchamp's *Portrait (Dulcinea)* and many other works in the Arensbergs' collection underwent restoration and cleaning by the Arensbergs' art restorer, Mary Ann Adler.

17. Adeline Fitzgerald reported that this "little gallery of camera portraits" also included "Braques [*sic*] photographed by Fritz Henle; Henri Matisse by his son Pierre, who caught the gray-bearded artist sitting in a row boat beside a pond with swans; 'Sandy' Calder and his wife, lounging in a pasture; Derain and Dalí, both by Man Ray; and Carlos Merida by Peter Pollock [*sic*] of the Institute staff" (*Chicago Sun-Times,* Oct. 21, 1949, AIC Ryerson).

18. Letter from Duchamp to the Arensbergs, Oct. 21, [1949], FBL. The only surviving visual documentation on the installation is Duchamp's drawing, which is reproduced in this article (fig. 9), and which was enclosed in this letter to the Arensbergs. Neither the early blueprints for the installation (mentioned in a letter from Kuh to the Arensbergs, Apr. 26, 1949, box 2, f. 9, PMA) nor photographs of the final installation, if indeed there were any, have been located.

19. Letter from Duchamp to the Arensbergs (note 18).

20. Frank Holland, "Free Art Lectures Back Arensberg Show," *Chicago Sun-Times,* Nov. 13, 1949, AIC Ryerson.

21. The series began a few weeks after the exhibition opened. Rich discussed "Modern Sculpture and Brancusi" (Nov. 4), and Kuh talked on "Marcel Duchamp, Pioneer" (Nov. 18). The two other lectures were entitled "Space and Painting" (Nov. 29) by artist/designer Serge Chermayeff, then president of Chicago's Institute of Design; and "Modern Art and Twentieth-Century Man" (Dec. 6) by Samuel I. Hayakawa, the future senator from California who was then a columnist for the *Chicago Defender* and a semiologist. Gallery talks, on various topics ranging from an overview of the collection to individual artists, Cubism, and avant-garde sculpture, were given by Kuh and Art Institute lecturers George Buehr, Helen Parker, and Dudley Crafts Watson.

22. Cable from Taylor to Walter Arensberg, Dec. 17, 1949, box 7, f. 22, PMA. In fact, despite his antipathy toward modern art, Taylor was interested in securing the Arensbergs' collection for the Metropolitan Museum. On Taylor's general dislike of modern and contemporary art, see, for example, his "Modern Art and the Dignity of Man," *Atlantic Monthly* 182, 6 (1948), pp. 30–36; and Calvin Tomkins, *Merchants and Masterpieces: The Story of the Metropolitan Museum of Art,* rev. ed. (New York, 1989), pp. 305–10.

23. Eleanor Jewett, "Modern Show in Last Week at Art Institute," *Chicago Tribune,* Dec. 11, 1949, AIC Ryerson.

24. While Ecke Bonk proposed that it was "likely. . .Duchamp worked on the selection and layout of the illustrations in the catalogue" (Bonk, *Marcel Duchamp: The Box in a Valise, de ou par Marcel Duchamp ou Rrose Sélavy,* trans. David Britt [New York, 1989], p. 311), in fact Duchamp's only involvement with the catalogue was to assist Katharine Kuh in verifying factual information on the artworks.

25. *Congressional Record* (81st Congress) 95, pt. 9, p. 11584. Alfred H. Barr, Jr., first director of New York's Museum of Modern Art, conjectured that the stigma of Dondero's accusation, though false, delayed the security clearance for Duchamp's United States citizenship; see letter from Barr to Nelson Rockefeller, Nov. 22, 1955, Alfred H. Barr, Jr., Papers, The Museum of Modern Art Archives (available in The Museum of Modern Art Papers, roll 2182, frames 122–23, AAA). The three other artists Dondero accused of being "reds" were Braque, Léger, and Picasso; the latter two were, in fact, affiliated with the Communist Party. For more on the accusation of Rich, see the essay by John W. Smith in this issue.

26. "An Interview with Katharine Kuh," ed. William McNaught, *Archives of American Art Journal* 27, 3 (1987), p. 25. See also Kuh, "Walter Arensberg and Marcel Duchamp" (note 9).

27. For more on Kuh's activities on behalf of modern art as a dealer, educator, and curator, see Avis Berman, "The Katharine Kuh Gallery: An Informal Portrait," in *The Old Guard and the Avant-Garde: Modernism in Chicago, 1910–1940,* ed. Sue Ann Prince (Chicago, 1990), pp. 155–69; and Susan F. Rossen and Charlotte Moser, "Primer for Seeing: The Gallery of Art Interpretation and Katharine Kuh's Crusade for Modernism in Chicago," *The Art Institute of Chicago Museum Studies* 16, 1 (1990), pp. 6–25.

28. For a detailed examination of these discussions, see Sawelson-Gorse, "'For the want of a nail'" (note 11), pp. 180–84.

29. Letter from Walter Arensberg to Kuh, Apr. 9, 1949, Katharine Kuh Papers, Beinecke.

30. The museum was supposed to be erected within five years after hostilities ceased with Nazi Germany following World War II. It was to house the Arensbergs' collection intact for twenty years, with only selected items allowed to be shown elsewhere, according to the provisions in the agreement between the Arensbergs, acting as trustees of the Francis Bacon Foundation, and the Regents of the University of California, Sept. 19, 1944.

31. Letters from Rich to Walter Arensberg, Sept. 13, 1939, and Sept. 1, 1948, box 2, f. 5 and f. 8, PMA.

32. Letter from Kuh to Daniel Catton Rich, undated, Katharine Kuh Papers, AIC Archives.

33. Ibid. Kuh was not the only one to suffer from this psychological game playing—so, too, did Walter's own staff. For example, several times he was known to have dismissed his research assistant Elizabeth Wrigley, only to telephone her that same evening (usually the call was made by Louise) and beg her to return.

34. Letter from Kuh to Rich, undated, Katharine Kuh Papers, AIC Archives.

35. Letter from Walter Arensberg to Rich, Oct. 14, 1948, box 2, f. 8, PMA.

36. Up until Kuh's last visit with the Arensbergs, in April 1949, however, the Arensbergs insisted upon including the African objects in the exhibition.

37. Letter from Louise Arensberg to Kuh, undated, Katharine Kuh Papers, roll 2225, frame 735, AAA.

38. Kuh's edition of Duchamp's 1934 *Green Box,* 169/300, which she donated to the Vassar College Art Gallery, Poughkeepsie, New York, in 1976, was one of at least five the Arensbergs owned; four (I/XX; 107/300; 167/300; and 168/300) are in the Louise and Walter Arensberg Collection, Philadelphia Museum of Art. *Monte Carlo Bond* of 1924, illustrated in this article (fig. 11), was given to Kuh by Rich, and then re-signed by Duchamp in 1953 with a personal dedication to her (see letter from Duchamp to Kuh, Jan. 22, 1953, Kuh Papers, Beinecke). Kuh donated the work in 1971 to The David and Alfred Smart Museum of Art at the University of Chicago. In 1965, she received *L.H.O.O.Q. Shaved* from the New York art gallery Cordier and Ekstrom; ten years later, she gave the item, by exchange, to the artist Clinton Hill.

39. Kuh's letters to the artists are preserved in her papers in the AIC Archives and in the Beinecke.

40. Letter from Kuh to Louise Arensberg, Sept. 15, 1948, box 2, f. 8, PMA. In addition to an essay on Duchamp that related to the Arensberg exhibition ("Four Versions of 'Nude Descending a Staircase,'" *Magazine of Art* 42, 7 [1949], pp. 264–65), Kuh wrote about her experiences with Duchamp and the Arensbergs ("Walter Arensberg and Marcel Duchamp" [note 9], pp. 56–64, an expanded version of an article first published in 1970 in *The Saturday Review*); participated with Duchamp and others in the panel discussion "Where Do We Go From Here?" at the Philadelphia Museum College of Art, Mar. 10, 1961; and interviewed Duchamp on Mar. 29, 1961 (Kuh subsequently published the interview in her book *The Artist's Voice: Talks with Seventeen Artists* [New York and Evanston, Ill., 1962], pp. 81–93).

41. Letter from Kuh to Louise Arensberg, Sept. 15, 1948 (note 40).

42. Kuh, "Walter Arensberg and Marcel Duchamp" (note 9), p. 57. Duchamp's gestures toward the Art Institute did not end with his assistance of Kuh regarding the Arensbergs' collection. He arranged for Rich and Kuh to see his *Bride Stripped Bare by Her Bachelors, Even (Large Glass)* (1915–23; Philadelphia Museum of Art). This pivotal, though incomplete, work, which the Arensbergs had once owned and for which they still retained many preliminary items, was then installed in the Connecticut home of Katherine Dreier, Duchamp's other great American patron.

43. The board was notified in a meeting on November 9, 1949, about two weeks after Marx's initial letter to the Arensbergs.

44. Kuh, telephone conversation with the author, May 8, 1991.

45. The Arensbergs also informed the Art Institute that they did not want to be interviewed, and that all publicity about the exhibition and catalogue be focused upon the artworks. While the Art Institute's staff respected their wishes, the Arensbergs themselves granted a request from Jules Langsner, the Los Angeles critic for *Art News,* to interview them extensively for an article in the journal; see "The Arensberg Riches of Cubism," *Art News* 47, 7 (1949), pp. 24–25, 61–62. For a description by Langsner of their difficult behavior during the interview process, see the letter from Langsner to Thomas Hess, Editor, *Art News,* Oct. 3, 1949, Jules Langsner Papers, roll 974, frames 9–10, AAA.

46. Letter from Louise Arensberg to Kuh, Oct. 26, [1949], Kuh Papers, roll 2225, frames 754–55, AAA.

47. Kuh, telephone conversation with the author, May 8, 1991.

48. Letter from Walter Arensberg to Duchamp, Apr. 8, 1950, FBL. The couple was also incensed that the frame on *The City* by Léger had been restored without their knowledge and that a Calder mobile had been damaged. The frame was repainted because of flaking paint. The mobile was broken by a visitor to the exhibition, but Calder later repaired it himself.

49. Letter from Walter Arensberg to Duchamp, Apr. 8, 1950, FBL.

50. Kuh asked to see the Arensbergs again in California, "both as a friend and also to revisit the paintings and sculpture with which (she) had worked so intimately and so happily," and was refused; letter from Kuh to Walter Arensberg, Dec. 13, 1950, box 2, f. 11, PMA.

51. On this acquisition, see letter from Duchamp to Kuh, Jan. 22, 1953, Katharine Kuh Papers, Beinecke; and "New Sculpture at the Art Institute," *The Art Institute of Chicago Quarterly* 47, 4 (1953), pp. 62–63. The Art Institute of Chicago, after the Philadelphia Museum and The Museum of Modern Art, New York, today boasts one of the most important representations of Brancusi's work in the United States.

52. Aline Louchheim, "The Arensbergs Bought Cubism Then," *New York Times,* Oct. 23, 1949; see also Langsner, "The Arensberg Riches of Cubism" (note 45).

53. Letter from Perls to Walter Arensberg, Oct. 16, 1949, box 10, f. 1, PMA. The exhibition provided the impetus for Walter Pach, the Arensbergs' first mentor, to write in the pages of a sketchbook his reminiscences of the couple—the impact of the Armory Show on them, and their capacity to maintain over many years their commitment to and interest in modern art. This section of Pach's "The Politer, the Cutt'n'er," which was part of a proposed article for *Harper's* magazine, was omitted from the final edited version published as "Art Must Be Modern," *Atlantic Monthly* 185, 5 (1950), pp. 44–48; the complete text is preserved in box 9, f. 15, PMA. For another critic who drew parallels between the 1913 and 1949 exhibitions, see Clarence J. Bulliet, "Arensberg Collection—Born in the Armory, Bows in Chicago," *Art Digest* 24, 3 (1949), pp. 7–8.

54. Letter from Peter Pollack to Alexander Eliot, Art Editor, *Time*, Sept. 12, 1949, Public Relations files, AIC Archives.

55. Letter from Peter Pollack to Clarence J. Bulliet, Art Editor, *Chicago Daily News*, Oct. 10, 1949, Public Relations files, AIC Archives.

56. On the Western Round Table, held at the San Francisco Museum of Art on April 8–10, 1949, see Bonnie Clearwater, "Trying Very Hard to Think: Duchamp and the Western Round Table on Modern Art, 1949," in Clearwater, ed. (note 4), pp. 46–59.

57. Ed Barry, "'Nude' Creator Quits Painting and Tells Why," *Chicago Tribune*, Oct. 20, 1949, sec. 3, p. 17; "Be Shocking," *Time* 54, 18 (Oct. 31, 1949), p. 42; and Cloyd Head, "In Our Town: Arensberg Collection of Modern Art," Oct. 23, 1949, AIC Archives. Bulliet mentioned the interview in his article about the opening of the exhibition ("Arensberg Gallery at Art Institute," *Chicago Daily News*, Oct. 20, 1949, p. 30), but no quoted statements were included.

58. See note 39 above.

59. Duchamp was not implying here that the Matisse works owned by the Arensbergs were forgeries. But he was apparently commenting on an aspect of the publicity that Matisse received in 1948–49, when two large retrospectives (at the Philadelphia Museum of Art and the Musée des Beaux-Arts in Lucerne) and many smaller shows were held in celebration of the artist's eightieth birthday, prompting published accounts regarding Matisse and forgeries. These do not mention falsely attributed works, so it remains unclear where Duchamp obtained information about plagiarism.

60. "Be Shocking" (note 57). A slightly different version of this quotation appears in Barry (note 57): "I might have an idea tomorrow for a picture, and use it."

61. Barry (note 57).

62. Ibid.

63. Duchamp here was certainly mocking the much publicized statement made by President Harry S. Truman, in a letter of April 2, 1947, to William Benton, Assistant Secretary of State, responding to criticisms of the United States Department of State's traveling exhibition, "Advancing American Art": "I am of the opinion that so-called modern art is merely the vaporings of half-baked, lazy people." The letter was quoted in numerous newspaper articles; see, for instance, Arthur Sears Henning, "Truman Gives Benton for His 'Art' Exhibition—Ridicules Modernism as Depicted by Reds," *Chicago Daily Tribune*, June 4, 1947. In his diary, Truman repeatedly used the word "lazy" to describe (and define) modern artists; see *Off the Record: The Private Papers of Harry S. Truman*, ed. Robert H. Ferrell (New York, 1982), pp. 129 and 336.

64. "Be Shocking" (note 57).

65. This question does not appear in the transcript, and Duchamp's following statement came at the end of his remarks on his paintings *Nude Descending a Staircase, No. 2*, and *The King and Queen Surrounded by Swift Nudes*.

66. A slightly different version was quoted by Barry (note 57): "After all, we're all ready to die."

67. "Be Shocking" (note 57).

68. Duchamp's recollection of the display of the works in the Arensbergs' Hollywood home was quite vivid; he had visited them the previous April. Some of the paintings were cleaned by the Arensbergs' restorer, Mary Ann Adler, before the exhibition; see note 16 above.

69. In 1915, when Duchamp first arrived in the United States, he stayed briefly with the Arensbergs in their apartment at 33 West 67th Street before moving into his own quarters. He then lived in a studio in their apartment building until 1918.

70. In Barry (note 57), this statement reads: "The title enriches your palette. . . .You add a new cerebral color that does not exist in the sunlight."

71. In fact, it was six months. Although the Arensbergs lent this work more frequently than any other, and it was displayed in the United States on numerous occasions, Duchamp rarely had the opportunity to see the painting after it was sent to the United States to be exhibited in the 1913 Armory Show. The three times he did see it were in 1920 (at the Arensbergs' New York apartment); in 1936 (at the Cleveland Museum of Art's "20th Anniversary Exhibition of the Armory Show"); and in 1949 (at the exhibition held at the San Francisco Museum of Art in conjunction with the Western Round Table in which Duchamp participated).

72. Apparently, this question was posed by Cloyd Head, according to the typed transcript of his radio broadcast; see Head (note 57), p. 6.

73. Duchamp appropriated the marble cubes for the piece from their usual cooking function "in kettles to prevent deposits of lime scale by their motion in. . .boiling water" (Bonk [note 24], p. 223 n. 1).

Editor's Acknowledgments

I would like to thank a number of people at the Art Institute who have contributed their time and efforts to this issue of *Museum Studies*. I am grateful to James N. Wood, President and Director, and Teri J. Edelstein, Deputy Director, for their continued support of the journal. My deep appreciation goes to Jack P. Brown, Executive Director of the Ryerson and Burnham Libraries, who read manuscripts and provided helpful advice. I also wish to thank archivists John W. Smith and Andrew Martinez for sharing their time and expertise so generously. As always, I am grateful to Robert V. Sharp and Katherine Houck Fredrickson of the Publications Department and Ann Wassmann of the Department of Graphic Services for their invaluable contributions. Cris Ligenza and Manine Rosa Golden of the Publications Department also helped in important ways. The Department of Imaging and Technical Services was involved at every stage in the preparation of this issue, and I wish to express particular appreciation to Alan Newman, Christopher K. Gallagher, Annie Morse, and Pam Stuedemann. As this issue was beginning to take shape, Margo Hobbs Thompson of the Department of Art History at Northwestern University did a prodigious amount of research on our behalf, and much of her work has found its way into these pages. Finally, my greatest debt is to Susan F. Rossen, Executive Director of Publications at the Art Institute, whose tenacity, wisdom, and hard work made possible this issue of *Museum Studies*. —M.S.

THE ART INSTITUTE OF CHICAGO (1992–93)

TRUSTEES

Mrs. Walter Alexander
Mrs. James W. Alsdorf
Jennifer D. Ames
Robert Bergman
John H. Bryan
A. Steven Crown
Mrs. Robert O. Delaney
Mrs. Thomas H. Dittmer
Wesley M. Dixon, Jr.
Marshall Field
Stanley M. Freehling
Michael Goodkin
Charles C. Haffner III
David C. Hilliard
Julius Lewis
Lewis Manilow
H. George Mann
Howard M. McCue III
John D. Nichols
Charles Price
Thomas J. Pritzker
Joseph Regenstein, Jr.
Andrew M. Rosenfield
Daniel C. Searle
James O. Silliman
Edward Byron Smith, Jr.
Mrs. Thomas S. Tyler
Mrs. Vernon M. Wagner
Dr. Karl J. Weintraub
Clarence S. Wilson, Jr.
Stephen M. Wolf

LIFE TRUSTEES

Mrs. Ivan L. Albright
Mrs. Frederic C. Bartlett
Edward H. Bennett, Jr.
Mrs. Edwin A. Bergman
Bowen Blair
Edward M. Cummings
Mrs. Eugene A. Davidson
Mrs. Edwin J. DeCosta
Maurice Fulton
William E. Hartmann
Neison Harris
John H. Johnson
Miss Louise Lutz
Mrs. Harold T. Martin
Mrs. Robert B. Mayer
Brooks McCormick
Andrew McNally III
Charles A. Meyer
John W. Moutoussamy
Bryan S. Reid, Jr.
Albert A. Robin
Mrs. Paul Rosenbaum
Mrs. Wolfgang Schoenborn
Arthur W. Schultz
Joseph R. Shapiro
Edward Byron Smith
Mrs. Theodore D. Tieken
Payson S. Wild
Arthur MacDougall Wood
William Wood Prince

EX OFFICIO HONORARY TRUSTEES

Richard M. Daley
Mayor, City of Chicago

Walter Knorr
Comptroller, City of Chicago

Richard A. Devine
President, Chicago Park District

Robert Penn
General Superintendent, Chicago Park District

EX OFFICIO TRUSTEE

James N. Wood
President and Director, The Museum of The Art Institute of Chicago

OFFICERS

Marshall Field
Chairman of the Board of Trustees

Stanley M. Freehling
Senior Vice Chairman of the Board of Trustees

John H. Bryan
Vice Chairman of the Board of Trustees and Treasurer

Mrs. James W. Alsdorf
Vice Chairman of the Board of Trustees

Wesley M. Dixon, Jr.
Vice Chairman of the Board of Trustees

James N. Wood
President and Director, The Museum of The Art Institute of Chicago

Robert E. Mars
Executive Vice President for Administrative Affairs

Larry Ter Molen
Executive Vice President for Development and Public Affairs

Phyllis L. Robb
Secretary